THIS BOOK
BELONGS TO
EDMONTON K

A Jew Returns Home

A Jew Returns Home

*A former interviewer for the BBC questions
Ben Ami, raised far from his heritage, about his
miraculous return to Judaism*

Sara Soester and Ben Ami

First published 2004
ISBN 0-9743911-4-X

Copyright © 2004 by JERUSALEM PUBLICATIONS

All rights reserved.

No part of this publication may be
translated, reproduced, stored in a retrieval
system, adapted or transmitted in any form or by any
means, electronic, mechanical, photocopying,
recording, or otherwise, without permission
in writing from the copyright holder.

Distributed by Feldheim Publishers
208 Airport Executive Park,
Nanuet, NY 10954
1-800-237-7149

JERUSALEM PUBLICATIONS
Jerusalem, Israel

10 9 8 7 6 5 4 3 2 1

Printed in Israel

With thanks and gratitude to *Avinu b'Shamayim*, our Father in
Heaven, Who enabled us to write our book
and Who brought us home.

And to our patient, understanding, enthusiastic
editor and friend, Mrs. Aviva Rappaport.
Thank you.

With gratitude to my dear long-suffering children.

To the **Chief Rabbi of Rehovot, Harav Simcha HaCohen Kook**,
and to his devoted **Rebbetzin Nechama**;
and to **Rabbi Chaim Walkin and his wife Henny** of Bayit VeGan,
whose influence helped me to become a true servant of Hashem.
To **Reverend Leslie and Mrs. Josie Hardman** of London,
who initially pointed me in the right direction.
To **Rabbi Yitzchak and Rebbetzin Henya Weinberg** of Vancover,
who continued the process.
To the **rabbis of Yad L'Achim**,
for their unfailing warmth and understanding.
To my very dear and wonderful friends in Rehovot, especially **Nini**,
my sounding board, and **Shoshy**, whose faith that
I could actually finish a book kept me going;
and to **Shelley**, who fed me magnificently almost every Shabbos.
To my special coauthor, **Ben Ami**, an outstanding Jewish mensch
in the truest sense of the word.

Sara Soester

✳ ✳ ✳

To my parents,
who gave me life,
and who, even as they shook their heads,
always stood by me.

To **Nathan**, and to **Dina**,
and the children of the Zs,
who taught me how to serve Hashem
and made me family.

To my dearest **wife** and partner
fulfillment of my dreams —
and to **our precious offspring**,
Jewish children, at home in *Eretz HaTzvi*.

✳ ✳ ✳

When Sara asked me if I would mind being interviewed to be included in a short chapter in a book she was writing, I readily agreed. Neither of us imagined that it would turn into such a project! I am grateful for the opportunity to have worked with her, and have come to appreciate her energy, her enthusiasm and her perseverance. Without her, this book never would have been written.
May Hashem give her many years of health and happiness…and the strength to write her own story.

Ben Ami

✳ ✳ ✳

Contents

1: The Menora	9
2: Jewish Identity	27
3: Rabbi Shimoni	36
4: *Hashgacha*	51
5: Purim	65
6: Shabbos	79
7: Governors Island	84
8: A Home for Shabbos	94
9: My "Yiddishe" Mama	100
10: Outreach Issues	108
11: Head Tales	146
12: Finding My Way	158
13: The *Siyum*	173
14: My Grandfather	181
15: The Search for Harav Yaakov Moshe	201
16: My Long-Lost Cousin	211
17: My Heart Is in the East	216
18: On My Way	228
19: Coming Home	246

1

"THE MENORA"

Q: When an irreligious Jew returns to Judaism, he treads a hazardous path. There are the feelings to consider of those who, though they cannot understand his change of heart, are still near and dear to him. He may have to endure the ridicule and perhaps the loss of former friends, Jews and otherwise, who may feel uncomfortable in his presence. He may even find that he has to give up his job if he does not want to violate the Sabbath. If the newly observant Jew decides to go and live in Israel, he will have to learn a new and difficult language, make new friends and adapt to a completely different way of life. For the Jew who has had some acquaintance with Judaism and Jewish customs, this is a daunting prospect. But for a Jew like you who grew up in a Christian home, and whose parents had left their Judaism far behind, the journey must have been traumatic.

A: Oh, it was. It was hard. It was very, very hard. But, of course, my return to Judaism did not take place overnight. It was a slow process that took place over a number of years.

Q: So let's go back to the beginning.

A: Well, strangely enough, the beginning of my journey back to Judaism started symbolically with a Chanuka menora — the same menora that marked my parents' last stop before leaving Judaism for Christianity.

My parents lived in Central Islip, Long Island, which was a predominantly non-Jewish area, and that is where I was born and where I grew up. There was virtually no anti-Semitism there to remind us that we were Jews. By the time my mother was twenty-five, she had five children, all under the age of seven. She was going through some sort of crisis, caused, I imagine, by physical and mental exhaustion. She married at seventeen and had all five of us, one after the other. She enjoyed being a mother, but I am sure we were quite a handful. She must have been asking herself, "Is this what life is all about? Running after a bunch of screaming children and changing diapers?"

One winter, just before Chanuka, she asked my father to buy a menora. My father must have wondered if he had heard her properly, since my mother came from a home where there was very little expression of Judaism. My father's background was, if anything, even weaker. Nevertheless, he told her if it would make her happy, he would get one.

Although I was only about three years old at the time, I clearly remember my father coming home and placing the menora on top of our large black-and-white television set in the living room. And each evening, we children, along with my mother, would gather around the TV as my father solemnly screwed another lightbulb into the electric socket. We didn't sing any songs. No blessings were said. Nothing was known about Chanuka. We just stood there staring at the menora, looking at the lights.

As you can imagine, it was not the most uplifting experience. It did nothing at all for my mother, or indeed for any of us. This was our first and last Jewish celebration as a family.

Q: But how did she get involved with the church?

A: One of my mother's neighbors was a Christian and a regular churchgoer. I do not know whether or not my mother confided in her, but somehow she knew that my mother was troubled. She invited her to church — a Baptist church — where my mother met some very warm and friendly people. In no time at all, my mother became the first Christian in our family.

Q: The Baptists are among the most experienced when it comes to drawing Jews into their Christian orbit. But what about your father? Didn't he say anything? Did he try to dissuade her from going?

A: It's hard for me to say. Don't forget that I was only about three at the time. The story I heard was that initially he was against it. But on the other hand, he saw that my mother was happy. He agreed to take her to the church and pick her up, but he would not leave the car. My mother's new friends made a point to go out to greet him. They were very friendly, and, in time, he joined her. Gradually, they became more and more involved in Christianity, and today, out of a family of seven — my mother, my father, my two brothers, my two sisters and myself — I am the only one who is a fully observant, totally committed Jew.

Q: Were your mother's parents still alive when your mother joined the church? How did they react to this?

A: My grandmother, my mother's mother, told me in the last week of her life that she realized she had only herself to blame. She admitted that she had not provided a Jewish education for her children, so what could she expect? Now that I have my own children, I understand this more and more clearly. If I want them to remain Jews, then I have to see to it that they understand that being Jewish is worth something. I have an obligation to give them a Jewish education. It is impossible to expect a child to feel strongly about Judaism — to feel pride in being Jewish — if you don't teach him these things. If you don't teach your child how to cross the street, he could be in a serious accident. By the same token, if you don't educate a child with Jewish values, you are almost guaranteeing that he will abandon the faith.

My mother did not abandon Judaism. She had nothing to abandon. She wasn't taught anything. My mother became a Christian because she wasn't taught to be a Jew.

Q: Isn't that a rather sweeping statement?

A: Yes, but I am certain it is true. I feel very strongly about this. An opportunity was squandered. When my mother was a young girl, she actually asked her mother to send her to an after-hours Jewish school with her neighborhood friends. She begged my grandmother to let her go. My grandmother agreed, but after a short while, she pulled her out of the school. That was the extent of my mother's Jewish education. Once out of the school, she associated more and more with the non-Jewish girls in the neighborhood.

Q: Why did your grandmother pull her out?

A: There was some kind of disagreement over the tuition, and my mother was taken out of the school. Her Jewish education ended right there.

Q: Even if your mother's parents took her out of the school, how could that have affected her to such an extent that so many years later she would turn to a different religion? Do you really think your mother is blameless in all this? What about free will? Where does that come in?

A: I am not in a position to apportion blame to anyone. Obviously, things are more complicated than that. Not everyone who has had such an experience is going to change his religion. The bottom line is that each person is responsible for his actions. However, I sincerely believe that it is up to the parents to provide their children with the proper tools to see them through the crises of life. My mother was in pain. She felt her life was meaningless. Had she received a Jewish education when she was young — the Torah, the Writings, the Prophets and the words of our Sages, which are the essential tools to make the right decisions — maybe she would never have fallen into the Christian trap.

How can you expect a child, or an adult for that matter, to make the proper moral and religious decisions without providing any guidelines? I liken it to a person dying of thirst. He sees a pool of polluted water and, with his last ounce of strength, he revives himself. But no one has told him that a sparkling freshwater spring is in his own backyard. Can you blame him when he is so grateful to have found the polluted water? It saved his life! In America, you often hear parents say, "I don't want to impose any type of Jewish ritual on my children. When they are old enough, they can decide for themselves."

Rabbi Bulman* used to say, "Would you say the same thing about teaching your children to eat with a knife and folk?" What about any of the other skills you need in life such as reading, writing, or crossing the street?

Q: What happened to your mother during the intervening years from the time she was pulled out of the Jewish class until she was twenty-five?

A: Jewishly speaking? Absolutely nothing!

Q: What about your father's family? You seem to speak almost exclusively of your mother's side.

A: I know more about my mother's side, but I wish I knew more about both.

Q: Today, your parents are active members in a Baptist church. Your mother teaches in the church school and in her younger days was the Sunday school superintendent. Your older brother is a Baptist minister. Your older sister is married to a minister and was a missionary in Nicaragua, or was it Guatemala?

---
* Harav Nachman Bulman, *ztz"l*

A: Actually, both.

Q: Whatever. Your younger brother, while nonreligious, views himself as part of the Christian world. Your younger sister is also married to a non-Jew. Yet you are a happily married observant Jew. Your extremely talented wife is *frum* from birth. Your beautiful little children are steeped in Judaism (*bli ayin hara*). Your life is so full of meaning! If you had the courage to get up and leave Christianity, why couldn't they? What prevents them? Why can't they see what you see?

A: Well, my case is different. Unlike my brothers and sisters, I came to see the emptiness and foolishness of Christianity and of American Western values. I discovered that my living as a Jew infused every moment of my life with meaning. I don't think you are right to assume that it is a lack of courage that prevents them from returning to a Jewish life. For them, it's not even in their consciousness, whereas I saw things differently.

Q: But why? You grew up with the same parents and grandparents. You grew up in the same home environment. What makes you so different?

A: Because not everyone experiences life in the same way. Two people can be in exactly the same environment, the same things can happen to both of them, and yet they will relate to their experiences in a different way. We all have our own unique goals and desires, with our own unique way of thinking, feeling and expressing ourselves. It is true that I grew up in the same house that my brothers and sisters grew up in, and it is true that we had the same parents and grandparents. But we responded to the world in totally different ways.

I don't really have an answer. I consider myself very fortunate, because for me there was always a tremendous amount of *hashgacha*. As I started and continued to identify as a Jew, I often felt the unseen hand of *hashgacha pratis* guiding me, sometimes pulling me, along the proper path. Even so, it was hard. The *kiruv* movement was already strong by the time I started to identify as a Jew, but I did not know of its existence. For a long time, I was very much alone as I started to make my way back to Judaism.

Q: What brought you back?

A: Let me see, it was around 1970. I was in junior high school, and a famous evangelist made a movie a few years after the Six Day War. The point of the film was to show that Jews were coming back to their land in fulfillment of Biblical prophecy. The main message was, of course, that the Jewish return is only a preliminary step leading to worldwide acceptance of Christian beliefs.

Q: That was the message?

A: Yes, that was the message. But the message for me was not the one intended. The sound track contained captivating music and songs, and there were lovely scenes of Israel, including the people of Israel. For the first time, I felt a sudden surge of pride, and I told myself, "These are my people!" I felt a part of them.

This was certainly amazing *hashgacha*. Imagine! This film was meant as an evangelistic tool, but for me it awakened my Jewish soul.

Q: Did you do anything about it?

A: No, not yet. The next stage did not come until a couple of years later in 1972, when I entered high school. The head of our English department was a former nun. It seems that whenever a nun or a priest left the Catholic Church, either from loss of faith, disillusionment, or whatever, she would hire him. My ninth grade English teacher, Miss Havers, a middle-aged woman, was one of those former nuns.

She was very concerned about anti-Semitism, and I guess this was one of the reasons why she had left the church. In any event, she requested permission from the high school principal to show the entire school a documentary about the Holocaust. I don't remember the name of the film, but I do remember that this was very unusual.

Q: What was so unusual?

A: It was almost unheard of in the early seventies for a public school — an American public school with a handful of Jewish families in the entire town — to show such a film. But she pushed it through. If

I close my eyes, I can still see myself sitting in the auditorium seeing the bodies...the bulldozers...the pits...the faces. The faces staring out at me from the screen could have been my very own family — my grandparents, my aunts and uncles. I was in shock.

Q: Why were you so shocked?

A: Because nobody talked about the Holocaust at home. I may have heard about it, but I didn't know what it was. Our family had been in America for generations. We were Americans. We didn't consider ourselves Jews at all. But what shocked me more than the images on the screen was what was going on in the school auditorium around me.

Q: Why? What happened?

A: As I was sitting there, absolutely shaken, stunned by what I saw, I could hear around me my friends, my non-Jewish fellow students, laughing. Looking back, I think that it was a nervous reaction of adolescents who did not know how to respond. But from that moment on, I felt that something separated me from them. I realized I was different from the non-Jew. Many years would pass before I understood that this marked a turning point: the beginning of my return to Judaism.

Q: Their laughter must have hurt your teacher very much.

A: I am sure it did, because after the film she told us

that anti-Semitism was a terrible virus, a virus of Western culture, and that all of us had to remember that we carry this virus within us. It is a virus that brings destruction, she told us emphatically, and that if we ever see it surfacing, we must do whatever we can to snuff it out. She was obviously very distressed by the students' reaction, and I remember that too.

Q: Did you go home after the movie and say to your parents, "I have just seen this documentary about the Holocaust, and I'm very upset by it"? Or was this subject taboo?

A: I really don't remember, but I do remember that after that I became obsessed with the subject. I read just about every book about the Holocaust that I could lay my hands on. For example, I remember reading *While Six Million Died*,* and I probably discussed this with my mother.

Q: It must have been very hard for you. Your mother and father were Jews, and yet they had left Judaism and embraced the teachings of the church. Christianity was largely responsible for the murder of six million Jews, including over one million infants, babies and small children. What did your mother say? What could she say? Did she feel guilty for turning her back on Judaism?

A: I don't think so. I remember her once saying, "Why

---

* *While Six Million Died, A Chronicle of American Apathy*, Arthur D. Morse (New York: The Overlook Press, New York, 1967).

do you have to take everything that happens as if it happens to you? Why do you have to feel so deeply about everything?"

Q: But how could she ignore the reality of over six million murdered Jews? Your Jewish lineage goes back thousands of years on both sides of the family.

A: But she didn't see it that way at all. For her the Holocaust and Christianity were totally separate issues because *those* Christians were not true Christians. True Christians don't kill Jews; they save Jews.

Q: How convenient: a theology that explains why the church leaders have never expressed their remorse or accepted their responsibility for what happened to the six million Jews in Christian Europe. It also explains how they can continue their aggressive proselytizing programs to the Jews, even in Israel. But I still can't understand how, given all this history, a Jew could become a Christian.

A: My mother related to those few Christians who rescued European Jews as the authentic representatives of Christianity. I agree with you that it is very convenient to evade the issue of Christians committing such atrocities by saying, "Well, they're just not true Christians." As I often told my mother, "It is a cop-out. It prevents an honest examination of how Christianity, despite its claims of brotherly love, has often been a force of destruction — and not only for Jews."

Q: Did your mother accept this?

A: Probably not. To her way of thinking, the Christian murderers were not a product of their beliefs but a perversion of them. Otherwise, how could she have turned to that same church?

Q: That's another subject. But what about you and your road back to Judaism?

A: That brings us to another interesting piece in the puzzle. In 1973, I was having pains in my leg, and it took a while before the doctors diagnosed the problem. They took X-rays, blood tests, and at first they thought I might have bone cancer. I underwent surgery. When they opened up my leg, some of the doctors wanted to amputate. However, the doctor in charge said, "Let's wait for the biopsy. Maybe its benign." As it turned out, it was benign.

For the first few months of my recovery I was unable to go to school, and two things happened. My mother used to listen to a Christian radio station. She particularly enjoyed a program where serialized versions of different Christian books were read. Naturally, stuck at home, I also heard this program. They happened to be reading from a book called *The Hiding Place.* The book was about a woman, Corrie Ten Boom, who, with her family, worked with the Dutch Underground during World War II. She, her father, her sisters, and her brother saved many Jews. Her brother and father died as a result. Corrie and her sister were sent to Ravensbruck, a concentration camp for women, and her sister died there. Her father was opposed to the Nazi regime, and he felt that, as a Christian, it was his duty to save Jews. As a result, the whole family was involved in rescue operations.

I saw Corrie Ten Boom as a heroic figure, someone I could look up to, someone who saved Jews. At that time, I still didn't know what it was to be a Jew, but somehow I felt a sense of appreciation because she and her family had risked so much to save my people, even though I still viewed myself as a Christian.

Over the next few years, she came to America on lecture tours, and I made a special effort to go and hear her. She wanted to demonstrate how belief in Christianity got her through the hellish experiences of the camps. The purpose of her talks was twofold: (1) to evangelize the unaffiliated to become "born-again" Protestant Christians, and (2) to strengthen the belief of those already committed. Little did she know that inside one of the "Christians" in the audience was a Jew trying to get out. With each of her talks that I attended, I felt a little more Jewish.

Getting back to my convalescence, while I was still on crutches and virtually homebound, my father bought me a shortwave radio to pass the time. Very soon, I discovered Kol Israel, the Voice of Israel, and it became my favorite radio station. I enjoyed listening to the English broadcasts, which were immediately followed by Hebrew broadcasts. Although I could not understand a word of Hebrew, I would not turn off the radio until the Hebrew broadcast had ended. I just had to hear those Hebrew words. And I was so frustrated because I could not understand what was being said.

Q: What did your parents think about your sudden immersion in things Jewish?

A: At this point, they didn't think anything because they didn't realize anything was going on. I myself didn't realize what was happening, either. I certainly did not think that this was the beginning of my return to Judaism. That realization came much later.

The next thing that happened was that an evangelical group decided to use Corrie Ten Boom's story as a vehicle for their missionary work. The idea was to produce a high-standard commercial film to be released in theaters. Until then, such films were openly evangelical, and were distributed through the churches. The goal here was to inspire the viewer to become a born-again Christian, not by hitting him over the head, but by showing how a devout Christian woman, because of her convictions, risked her life to save Jews. The evangelical message was there, but it was more subtly presented. It was only toward the end of the film that the evangelical message got strong.

Q: What about the Jews? Where did they come in all

this? These groups have special programs to evangelize the Jews, and I can not see them missing any opportunity to convert them.

A: I don't think Jews were specific targets, but as I recall, the film was advertised as a movie that Jew and Christian alike must see. It was a very slick job. This was the first evangelical film to use professional Hollywood actors, and it cost them a lot of money. The group appealed for contributions to finance the film. Their slogan was, "Become a member of the Hiding Place family!" and I actually contributed a lot of money. They sent newsletters to inform us "family members" of the film's progress. I felt a part of it. At the same time, the Jewish content further awakened the early stirrings of my self-identification as a Jew.

Q: You sound like you were suffering from a spiritual split-personality disorder.

A: I guess I was. I identified with the Jews. I identified with the production. It made me feel better.

Q: How could it possibly have made you feel better?

A: On the one hand, I thought of myself as a Christian. On the other hand, I felt more and more a Jew. I understood that, in fact, I was already moving away from Christianity, but I was frightened. I was not ready to abandon Christianity. Corrie Ten Boom's empathy for Jews enabled me, for a while, to avoid the issue, much as I think my mother has avoided it until this day. True

Christians didn't kill Jews; they saved them.

Anyway, the film came and went, but I remained very interested in the Jews. According to Protestant teachings, Jewish history ended when they rejected the Christian "savior." Jews were swallowed up by a black hole. Now, with the return of Jews to Israel, they have readmitted us to history. I started to ask myself what had happened to the Jews while the Christians had exiled them from history. And so, I started to expand my horizons by reading more and more about the history of the Jews. The more I read, the more I understood. The Corrie Ten Booms were vastly outnumbered by the people who didn't do anything, or worse, who contributed to the mass murders over the centuries. Christians say, "You know a tree by its fruit," and I said to myself, "What rotten fruit! What does that say about the tree? What does that say about Christianity?" At that point I started to, as they say, "have me doubts."

2

"Jewish Identity"

Q: The conflict must have been very hard on you.

A: Well, it wasn't as drastic as all that, because these were only the first stirrings. I continued to listen to the Hebrew broadcasts on Kol Israel on a regular basis, and this awakened a tremendous desire to learn the language.

I remember that even as a child, when we drove past the Williamsburg section in New York City, and I would see the signs with Hebrew letters, I would ask my father, "Daddy, what do the signs say?" He would reply, "I don't know." And I would say, "But you grew up Jewish. You should know!"

I continued reading about Jewish history as much as possible and, as a result, became curious about the Jewish holidays, in particular, how they compared with the Christian holidays. I was talking about this with a friend in church when somebody passed us, heard us talking, and hissed, "Why would anyone be interested in all THAT?"

I was becoming increasingly aware of the anti-Semitism in the church. I had more or less stopped going there regularly, and I gave up teaching in the children's Sunday school.

Q: Weren't your parents devastated by your doubts about their cherished beliefs?

A: Well...at that point they still had hopes that this was a phase, and that hopefully it would pass.

Q: Did they try to convince you to return to the church?

A: No. They didn't really know what was going on. It wasn't as if I stopped going to the church we grew up in. Things were different. My father had meanwhile joined the Coast Guard, and we moved to Governors Island. This meant that my parents were now attending the church on the Island, so they thought I simply didn't like that church.

Meanwhile, I decided to get down to the business of learning Hebrew. I had bought some Berlitz language records, but it was not going very well. I also tried learning from a book at some point, but that wasn't successful either. I basically had given up, but *hashgacha pratis* stepped in.

Soon after we moved to Governors Island, I saw an ad in *The New York Times*. The World Zionist Organization was offering an *ulpan*, a Hebrew language class. When I told my mother of my plans to enroll during the summer break, she said slowly, "Oh. I don't think you should go."

"Why?" I asked.

She said, "Well, you are a Christian, and if they find out you are a Christian, they will probably say nasty things to you. Your father and I don't want you to be hurt."

I told my mother, "Yeah, but I really want to learn Hebrew, and this is the only way I am going to learn it." I assured my mother that I would not volunteer the information that I was a Christian, but if anybody asked me, I wouldn't deny it, either. And so I went to the *ulpan*.

Q: Did you feel Jewish with all the Jews there, or did you still feel like a Christian?

A: Well, that is the amazing thing. In retrospect, I can see that the whole series of events was *hashgacha pratis* — my father joining the Coast Guard, our moving to New York City, my seeing the notice in *The New York Times*, my enrolling in the *ulpan*.

I really felt that the *ulpan* was a turning point. Here we were, a group of people all struggling to learn Hebrew, and therefore we enjoyed a certain camaraderie. I felt very comfortable. Within a few weeks, I felt much more comfortable with this group of people than with the people I had grown up with. I felt a real sense of belonging. I still had no idea where all this was going to take me. I felt very different. I felt very close to these people. I started to really identify as a Jew.

Q: What do you mean you started to identify as a Jew? I thought you still regarded yourself as a Christian.

A: Well, I suppose I was no longer a sterling example of a Christian. I guess I wasn't exactly a sterling example of a Jew either — but I was probably still a better Christian than Jew, because with Christianity you really don't have to do anything. You just have to believe. I still more or less believed that Christianity had superseded Judaism, with all the beliefs that entailed.

Q: It sounds as if you had a foot in each camp.

A: Looking back, I suppose I did, because I was in transition. At the time, however, I was still telling myself that I was a Christian with a great interest in Judaism and with a great affinity toward Jews.

There was one woman in our *ulpan* who was pretty amazing. She saw through this. She was a Hungarian Holocaust survivor. She had never married, and lived near Central Park with her two unmarried sisters. Although she was somewhat eccentric, she was charming. She was not a Hebrew scholar. She had been in the same class and level for many years.

Late one afternoon, I went for a walk in Central Park before class, and I saw her sitting on a bench. We exchanged greetings, and she beckoned me to sit down. We had some time before class began, and she told me a little about herself. She then asked me about my background, my education, and if I went to a Jewish school.

I braced myself. *Okay!* I thought. *The moment of truth has arrived. She is asking me directly, and it is wrong to lie.*

Taking a deep breath, I said to her, "I don't have any special Jewish education. My grandparents are Jewish, but I am a Christian."

Without missing a beat, she said, "Oh! So learning Hebrew is your way of coming back to us, isn't it? Why else would you want to learn Hebrew?"

I said to her, "Well, Hebrew is the language of the Bible, and it's our Bible too, and also my ancestors spoke the language, and I have no intention of—"

"Oh no," she broke in. "You're mistaken. You don't know it yet, but you want to come back to us, and this is your first step."

Of course, I thought she was just a crazy old

woman. Later on, as I became friendlier with the group, a few more people found out about my background. Someone in a different class overheard me talking about it to someone in our group and made a snide remark about my being a traitor to Judaism. The elderly survivor came to my defense, saying, "He has more Judaism in his little finger than you have in your entire body. It's just waiting to come out!"

Anyway, by the end of the semester, I was totally confused. I didn't know who or what I was anymore. I didn't know what I should do. I didn't know if I wanted to be a Christian, and I didn't know if I wanted to be a Jew. On the one hand, I was drawn to Judaism, but I wasn't sure if it was because I felt so much at home with my new Jewish friends or because I had lost my faith in Christianity.

I needed to sit by myself, to think and to decide what I wanted to do with my life. I decided not to enroll in the *ulpan* for the following semester.

After taking a break from my Hebrew studies I opened up the "New Testament" and tried to look at it objectively to see if it really made sense. I started from the beginning, paying particular attention to their quotes from the Five Books of Moses, and quickly discovered that they had taken the Hebrew scriptures completely out of context. Not only didn't their interpretations make sense, but there were blatant mistakes. The whole structure started to collapse in front of my eyes. I wondered how I could have possibly believed in all that. I wondered how anyone could possibly believe in all that.

Q: But how did you know enough about Judaism to make the comparison?

A: Actually, it didn't take too much knowledge, and that really surprised me. All it takes is reading with an open mind. I could give you example after example, and I think there are now *kiruv* people who are trained to do just that. As I turned each page, it struck me as so much hogwash.

Q: But how is it Christians today don't know about these mistakes? Hasn't anybody told them? Surely there must be some who have read the text as carefully as you did.

A: I don't know. They say it can't be understood in the simple sense. They paper things over. They try to ignore the discrepancies. It's not at all like Jewish study, where seeming inconsistencies are not only examined and pored over, but are studied with enthusiasm.

In any case, my doubts were accumulating at an ever-increasing rate. Meanwhile, my older brother, the Baptist minister, was living in Massachusetts, and we started up a rather active correspondence. I did not share my doubts with him. Our letters were more about the Jewish origins of Christianity, which interested him as well.

At about the same time, my sister had taken a

break from her missionary work in Central America and was visiting Canada. She had met someone there, and they had decided to get married. My brother was asked to officiate at the wedding, which would be held in the church on Governors Island, and I was enlisted to be the best man. In deference to my grandparents, I told my brother that perhaps he should tone down the Christian stuff in the ceremony and even introduce a bit of Jewish content. He thought it was a great idea, so much so that he even started practicing the priestly blessing in Hebrew.

The night before the wedding, we were reviewing what he planned to say. I kept telling him, "Don't say that! I think you could say this…" Finally, he said to me in exasperation, "Don't you think you're getting a little carried away with all this Jewish business? After all, we are Christians. You are a Christian, aren't you?" I gulped. He continued, "Maybe you should stop reading so much about Judaism and Jewish history. I can see you are becoming confused."

I thought for a moment, and said to him, "You know, I think that as time goes by I am actually becoming less and less confused."

That night, I couldn't sleep. I kept tossing and turning, worrying and wondering. For the first time, I started seriously thinking about my family's future.

Here was my sister, marrying a goy, a nice enough

fellow but nonetheless, not Jewish. I asked myself, "Why do I feel so uneasy about this wedding? Why should it bother me so much?" I wondered, "Who am I? What am I?"

The next morning when I got up, I knew the answer. I was no longer a Christian. I was a Jew.

3

"RABBI SHIMONI"

Q: Did you feel as if you had thrown off a huge burden?

A: Well...yes and no. I felt...I felt like...I was still plagued with doubts. It was a long process. I didn't know what being a Jew means.

Q: But that was hardly surprising, because you had no one to teach you or to guide you.

A: That was about to change. I was studying toward my master's degree at Rutgers University, and traveling back and forth each day from Governors Island to New Jersey. Rutgers had not been my first choice. I wanted to go to Johns Hopkins in Maryland, but one of my professors was late in sending a required letter of recommendation, so I could not be considered for the current academic year. Naturally, I was upset at her negligence, but as it turned out this was another incident of *hashgacha pratis*.

I listened to the radio a lot while driving to Rutgers and discovered a small college radio station with a few hours of Jewish programming each morning. One segment was called *Morning Chizuk* with Rabbi Dovid Goldwasser, who gave over a *devar Torah*. It was my first experience hearing a rabbi, and I was very impressed.

Q: What in particular impressed you?

A: It was not so much what he said, but how he said it. You see, I had been taught that Judaism was a dry legalistic religion. I was told that religious Jews did things by rote, without feeling. They supposedly just go through the motions, like robots, observing rituals without feeling, except perhaps fear, and mindlessly do what the rabbis tell them. That was always the impression I was given of the Jewish religion. Rabbi Goldwasser spoke with such tremendous enthusiasm and conviction. I felt betrayed.

Q: Betrayed? Why? By whom?

A: By the church, which presented Judaism as a religion that had not only lost its relevance, but was actually...uh...

Q: Dead?

A: Yes, quite dead.

Q: I know that Arnold Toynbee, the famous Christian historian, claimed that Judaism was a "fossilized civilization."* But I didn't realize that Christianity considers Judaism dead.

A: Yes — and that Christianity has replaced it.

Q: What was it about Rabbi Goldwasser that convinced you that the church's representation of Judaism as a dead religion was wrong?

A: It was his excitement. It was his energy. You could hear it in his voice. He was not merely reading from a script. This was real. It was as if he himself was actually experiencing, living, bringing to life the words of the texts he quoted. It was clear to me that his commitment to Judaism was anything but

---

* Dr. Yaakov Herzog, rabbi, lawyer, Talmudic scholar, statesman, then Israel's ambassador to Canada, debated Toynbee at Montreal's McGill University on January 31, 1961. Dr. Herzog was roused to indignation by the verdict of the world-famous historian concerning the essential nature of Jewry since the overthrow of the Hasmonean dynasty. In fact, the entire life of the Jewish Diaspora from 132 years after the advent of Christianity was defined by Toynbee as "a fossilized relic of an obsolete culture that no longer has either the power of continuity or the right to exist." (See then President of Israel Zalman Shazar's eulogy for Dr. Chaim Herzog in *A People That Dwells Alone*, Weidenfeld and Nicolson, 1975.)

rote or going through the motions. I realized that I was listening to a Jew who believed in G-d, a rabbi who passionately followed the commandments because G-d had commanded him to do so. So strong was the impression he made, I can still hear his voice in his sign-off saying, "This is Rabbi Goldwasser from *Morning Chizuk*. Have a nice day!"

Years later, I met Rabbi Goldwasser at a wedding, and I had the opportunity to thank him and to tell him how influential his program was in my returning to Judaism. He was very pleased.

Q: How did your increasing knowledge of Judaism affect your feelings about Christianity?

A: Well, I was becoming more and more skeptical. I felt that I had been lied to about the nature of Judaism. They had fed me this garbage about how dead it was. "Why are they afraid to admit that Judaism is a living religion?" I asked myself. "Who knows what other lies they are perpetuating?"

Q: What do you mean you were becoming more and more skeptical? Hadn't you already decided on the morning of your sister's wedding that you were no longer a Christian, that you were a Jew?

A: It was a progression. First, I stopped going to church. The second stage was an increasing revulsion toward Christianity. I said to myself, "Even if there were something to this nonsense, it would still be more of a hell to be in heaven with the Christians than to go to hell with the Jews."

Q: You really felt that?

A: Oh yes. The next stage was helped along by Rabbi Goldwasser's program. I began to see the beauty of Jewish concepts and texts. At this point, I never considered the possibility of becoming a religious Jew. Not at all. It was so far removed from my experience that it never even entered my mind. I was not yet ready to do something "Jewish" other than resume my Hebrew classes. I was beginning to feel comfortable with my new identity — not an observant Jew, but a Jew nonetheless. I probably could have remained this way for years, but *hashgacha pratis* was not about to leave me in peace.

Q: What happened?

A: One morning, I was driving to class at Rutgers University, and there was a massive traffic jam. I saw a small side street and decided to turn into it in the hopes of getting to class on time.

About a block down, I saw a small store on the left with a Hebrew sign saying, *Sefarim* — Books. "Wow, what a coincidence!" I said to myself. "Maybe I can buy the book I need for my *ulpan* there." The books used in the *ulpan* were sold in the building of the Jewish Agency in Manhattan. Driving into Manhattan in the middle of the day was not appealing. "With a little bit of luck," I said, "this detour may have saved me a lot of time." Very often, when things don't work out the way you want, you see later on that it just had to be that way. I wish I could learn this lesson better and apply it to the present, but it's much easier to apply it to the past.

After class, I retraced my route, and found the bookstore. I asked the woman behind the counter if she had the book I needed. She told me she didn't have it, but that her husband travels to New York once a week to buy books, and, if I could wait, he would have it for me next week.

She saw that I wasn't wearing a yarmulke and that I was a young guy, and she asked me why I was interested in learning Hebrew. "Did you learn any Hebrew in a day school when you were younger?" I later realized this question was probably her way of determining whether or not I was Jewish.

"Actually," I answered, "I never had any sort of Jewish education. My family is Jewish, but let's say we are very assimilated. Nevertheless, I always wanted to learn Hebrew, and I go once a week to an *ulpan* in New York. That's why I have to get that book."

"You know, " she said, "you really must meet my husband. He was born in Yemen but grew up in Israel. He can help you with your Hebrew. He's in the store on Thursday nights while I am busy preparing for Shabbat. Why don't you come next Thursday, and hopefully he'll have gotten the book for you by then."

The following Thursday, I returned to the shop.

Her husband, Rabbi Shimoni, was there, and I introduced myself.

"Oh, my wife told me you might be coming, but I'm very sorry. I wasn't able to get you the book. I'll do my best to have it for you next week."

I turned to leave, but he stopped me. "If you're already here, why not stay a while, and we can chat? My wife told me that perhaps I could help you with your Hebrew." We talked for a while, and he taught me a few words in Hebrew.

As we parted, he said, "You know, it would be nice for me if you would come Thursday nights on a regular basis. The store is never that busy, and I could use the company. I'm willing to help you with your Hebrew."

"Well," I answered, "I don't know. I live quite far from here, and I don't know if it would work out."

"So think about it," he said. "Anyway, come next Thursday to pick up the book."

I returned the following Thursday.

"Oh, I'm really sorry," he said apologetically, "but I don't have the book."

I stayed a while. There was a kosher pizza place just around the corner, and I went out and bought some pizza for us. We sat and chatted away, and he taught me some more Hebrew.

What do you think happened the following Thursday?

Q: He still didn't have the book! Did you ever get it?

A: I was getting annoyed. I enjoyed talking with him, but weeks were going by. Finally, in desperation, I said to him, "Listen, I'll continue our weekly visits even if you get the book!"

Q: Did you tell him about your background?

A: Not immediately. I just told him that I came from a family about as assimilated as you can get.

These weekly visits continued for about two years, and as we got to know each other better, I opened up more to him.

Q: Were your parents aware of these Thursday night meetings?

A: Yes.

Q: What did they say about it? Obviously, your interest in Judaism was getting more serious. Weren't they worried?

A: I don't think they were that worried. They were still nursing hopes that this was a passing phase. As time went on, however, my mother did become more concerned. One day she said to me, "So! You have all these questions. Why do you think you have all the answers? Some of the greatest minds over the centuries were Christian. Do you think you know something they didn't know? You were close to the minister from our church back on Long Island. Why don't you go and discuss your problems with Christianity with him?"

The truth is that I did admire the man and even considered him a trustworthy friend. He and his wife had always been very kind to me. He was always encouraging my interests even in areas other than religion, such as astronomy. He knew I was an astronomy buff, and one cold winter night when I was about nine years old, he brought his telescope over to our house to show me Saturn's rings.

I decided my mother was right. What harm could there be in speaking to him? Actually, I looked forward to seeing him again.

When I arrived at their house, his wife greeted me with a scowl rather than the warm smile I had always received in the past.

She directed me into the living room and told me to sit down while she called her husband. She pointed toward a large a platter of brownies on the coffee table. "I remember," she said, "how you used to love my brownies, but now that you're Jewish, I guess you wouldn't touch them, so I won't bother offering them to you."

Actually, I wasn't yet observant, but somehow I had lost my appetite anyway.

Q: What a childish reaction! Was the minister as openly hostile?

A: No, not at all. He asked me what was bothering me. I told him that, among other things, I had become aware of the anti-Semitism inherent in Christian teachings.

He agreed that while there were Christian anti-Semites, he could not agree that Christianity itself was anti-Jewish. He said that, in fact, his being a Christian caused him to be very concerned about Jews and Israel.

I was not pleased with this answer, because I knew the hidden agenda behind this concern. I told him that I found the reaction of Christians to events in Israel extremely offensive. Violence and terrorism against Jews were often cause for glee. They would enthuse, "Oh, this is a sign of the Second Coming! We are in the End of Days!" I also told him that it bothered me very much that Christianity claims to be a religion of love but this love is very exclusive. I asked him, "How is it possible that Christians can have so much love for one Jew, and have shed countless tears over his death for over two thousand years, and yet they haven't shed even one single tear for the Jewish people? This evangelical concern has nothing to do with concern for people. The real concern is that the Jews should play their part as pawns in some end-of-days eschatological drama."

Terrorism for them is a "sign of the times." How much thought was given to the mother, a daughter of Holocaust survivors who, hiding in a closet, smothered her own child while trying to cover her mouth to prevent her screams? How much thought was given to her husband, who before being cruelly murdered, was forced to watch their other daughter killed before his eyes? Parents? Children? They had all been transfigured into signs of the Second Coming! "These are Jews," I told him, "not signs!"

He thought about it for a moment and said, "You are right. Sensitivity is often missing. However," he went on, "this lack of empathy is not only expressed toward Jews. When there is an earthquake anywhere you find that some Christians also get very excited, seeing it as a sign of the Second Coming. The Bible predicts that there will be earthquakes, cataclysms, upheavals and wars before the end times. People will suffer."

I confessed, "The fact that Christians also get excited when peasants are wiped out by a typhoon in East Timor doesn't make me feel any better."

We ended our discussion with me more convinced than ever that there was absolutely nothing for me there.

Q: What was happening at home? Did you feel more and more alienated from your family as you started feeling closer and closer to Judaism? Was it an open conflict, or an uneasy truce?

A: It was easier than you might think. I was really very fortunate. For many years my mother was not on speaking terms with her mother. At the time of my parents' conversion, my grandmother was furious to the point where she refused to speak to them for many years until a reconciliation, of sorts, took place. This hurt my mother very much, and she made every effort to avoid hurting me in the same way. She objected to the path I had chosen, but she did so in a very careful and loving way. She understood that this was my decision and didn't push me hard at all. My father followed my mother's lead.

Q: What about your siblings? How did they react to the situation?

A: The one who reacted most negatively was my older brother, the Baptist minister. Once I began to openly identify as a Jew, our relationship deteriorated rapidly. For years after, there was very little communication between us. He told me I had betrayed him. He said, "You are attacking me and everything I believe in. It's my whole life — it's what I do — and you are telling me that it is not legitimate."

Since then, our relationship has improved considerably. When Jeanette and I were married, he came to our wedding in Eretz Yisrael. He was very respectful of us and commented on the commitment of the *kehilla* to which we belong. He even remarked that he had never seen such commitment in a church community.

Q: But didn't you say that one of the things that attracted your mother to the church was the warmth she found in the community?

A: There is a difference between warmth and commitment. It doesn't take much effort to smile at a newcomer. It takes a lot of effort to come day after day, devoting hours and hours to prayer and learning. My mother was never really exposed to that. My brother experienced firsthand the devotion to G-d evident in our community and the level of religious involvement in our ordinary lives.

He and my father spent the Shabbos after our wedding with us. We first went to shul for Mincha, *kabbalas Shabbos*, a "sermon," and Maariv. The next morning, we got up, not pausing to even eat, went to shul for about three-and-a-half hours for another service, a "sermon," and learning afterward. Then, home for kiddush, a meal with Shabbos songs and discussions on the weekly Torah portion. After a short rest, it was back to shul for Mincha, another *shiur* during *seudat shelishit*, the afternoon meal, and we finally closed the Shabbos with Maariv and havdala. And we were not finished yet. It so happened that that week we also said *kiddush levana*, the prayer for the sanctification of the new moon.

Q: Your brother must have been absolutely astounded!

A: I thought that when he saw us all praying and dancing in the moonlight he would think we had gone completely mad, maybe from sitting so much in shul. On the contrary, though, he was very impressed. I thought the long service might have been too much for him, but it wasn't. He very much enjoyed sitting in a tallis, wearing a *kippa*, and trying to follow in the siddur, with the rudimentary Hebrew he had learned in seminary. I think he would have liked the prayers to go on even longer!

He complained about the difficulty of getting his congregation to sit for even an hour. He had to make his sermons short and peppered with humor to keep his flock's attention.

The visit made such an impression on him that even years later he told me that he wondered how he could bring the beauty of our Shabbos to his community.

Q: Perhaps he'd have an easier time if he just brought himself to our community. How did your other siblings react to the changes in your life?

A: I was always very close to my older sister. Her reaction was very different. She thought I was making a mistake, a very big mistake, but that didn't affect our relationship at all.

Q: Were they worried that you would go to Gehinnom?

A: At that point, perhaps my brother wished I would! Seriously, I am sure they did. My older sister loves me, but I am afraid she believes that I will end up burning in hell.

Q: What about your younger siblings?

A: They are not really religious, so I don't think it matters so much to them. Actually, it's interesting though, the distribution in our family. The older children became very "religious" — very good Christians. I became a very religious Jew. The younger ones weren't interested in any religion at all.

Q: It really sounds very much as if each member of your family was doing pretty much their own thing, which is why perhaps your activities vis-à-vis Judaism simply passed them by.

4

HASHGACHA

Q: There is so much that a newcomer to Judaism must learn. How did you start?

A: At one of my weekly visits to the bookstore, Rabbi Shimoni told me I should really start by learning about the Jewish holidays. He suggested Eliyahu Kitov's *The Book of Our Heritage.**

"I have two editions for sale," he told me, "softcover and hardcover. I wouldn't buy the softcover one

---

* *The Book of Our Heritage: The Jewish Year and Its Days of Significance* (Feldheim).

if I were you. You will be using this set for many, many years. It will fall apart. Buy the hardcover edition. It's a better buy in the long run, believe me. You probably think I want to sell you something more expensive, but in the end it will save you money."

Well, since I was a student without too much money to spare, I bought the less expensive edition. Here it is.

Ben walked over to his bookcase, picked out a rather battered book and put a volume of The Book of Our Heritage on the table. As he put it down, some of the pages slowly fell to the floor.

"You see," he said as he picked them up, "I should have listened to him."

Q: What did Rabbi Shimoni think of your progress or lack of progress? Did you ever feel he was pushing you? Did he tell you to keep kashrut or anything like that?

A: No. He was not pushy. After I had known him for close to two years, he asked me, "What do you consider yourself now, a Christian or a Jew?"

When I told him that I felt I was a Jew, he said, "You know, you are used to the Christian way of thinking, where the main emphasis is belief. Just believe — you don't have to do anything. For Jews, though, belief is not enough. Hashem has given us commandments, and you have to act on them."

Rabbi Shimoni confronted me with this challenge at about the same time my life was about to undergo a major change.

Q: What change was that?

A: I had become disenchanted with university life. I decided to leave the university because I was very disturbed by the dishonesty I saw in the academic world: plagiarism, manipulation or falsification of data, publication of results known to be incorrect. This distressed me to a great degree. My decision came as a tremendous surprise to the professors in the department. I had completed the course work for my PhD. I was one of the top students and easily outperformed everyone else on the qualifying examination, and my research project was well funded. Things could not have been going better! Even so—

Q: I'm sorry to interrupt but isn't this dog-eat-dog atmosphere an integral part of the secular academic world? From my experience, it's a question of survival of the fittest — or toughest, or meanest. Nevertheless, it must have been a very hard decision for you to make, and even more so since everything was going your way, and you were so close to your goal.

A: It was, but I decided I couldn't remain there any longer. The blatant academic dishonesty was making me ill. To this day, one of the things I cannot tolerate at all is dishonesty. In fact, one rabbi once told me that the reason I came back home to

Judaism is that my *neshama* could not tolerate the deceit and perfidy that I saw in Christianity.

I stayed at Rutgers until the end of the semester, and then took a leave of absence. That was twenty years ago! I landed a job, but before I started it, I took a few weeks off to go to—

Q: Israel?

A: Israel! I convinced myself it was just a sightseeing trip. It was not a pilgrimage, and it was not a search for roots. I went to Yad Vashem; I spent a lot of time walking around Jerusalem, especially the Old City. I visited the Church of the Holy Sepulchre, because back then, I had no idea Jews are not allowed to enter churches. I almost went up to the Temple Mount. As you know, but I didn't know then, Jews are in a state of ritual impurity, and are not allowed to enter the site. When I approached the entrance, I saw the sign from the Chief Rabbinate warning that entry is prohibited to Jews. *Well*, I thought, *I'm a Jew, so I guess it's prohibited for me to go up there.*

So I didn't go. I didn't feel a surge of Jewish self-identity. It was just obvious to me that I shouldn't go.

Q: Were you the same person when you finished your tour of Israel as when you started the trip? Personally, I don't think that any Jew, however far from Judaism he may be, can come to Israel and not feel something, especially on seeing the

Western Wall for the first time.

A: Actually, my first sight of the *Kotel* was very disappointing. I entered the Old City with great anticipation. After all, I was going to see the Wall. I walked across the Jewish Quarter and went down the stairs to the huge plaza in front of the *Kotel*.

I felt nothing! Absolutely nothing! It was just a high old wall. I was shocked. I had expected to feel something. Amazement. Astonishment. But nothing happened. I stood looking at it, but something prevented me from even wanting to approach it. I walked away.

Q: Why? What was stopping you?

A: I guess I felt inadequate, unworthy. I was so upset that the expected rise of emotion was absent. I did not want to force an emotion that was not genuine. So I left.

But I had a problem. A religious friend in my *ulpan* had given me a note to place between the stones of the *Kotel*. I still had it, and I had to take care of it. I returned Friday afternoon, the last Friday before I would return to the States. It was close to Shabbos. I saw hundreds of Jews streaming in from the Jewish Quarter, making their way down to the *Kotel*. Everyone was dressed in their Shabbos best. Children were skipping across the plaza; little boys were tightly clutching the hands of their fathers. Columns of young yeshiva boys converged, holding hands, dancing and singing, as they made their way toward the Wall. The sun was setting, bathing the Wall in a golden light. There was an air of palpable excitement that was contagious. I didn't know it then, but I felt Shabbos. I saw the people, and I felt that this is what makes the place holy. I was overwhelmed. I approached the Wall with genuine emotion, and deposited my friend's note.

After I returned to America, I realized I had to do something in a practical way to demonstrate that I was a Jew. I resolved to keep "modified kosher."

Q: What in the world is "modified kosher"?

A: For me, it meant that I wasn't going to eat outright *treif*.

Q: How did you know what *treif* was?

A: I knew this even as a child. My mother's parents were not religious, but they wouldn't eat non-kosher meat. Whenever they came to visit us, my mother would buy kosher meat. She would cook it in our *treif* oven, and my grandparents would eat it. So, I adopted their "modified kosher." It may seem silly, but for me at the time, it was no trifling matter.

Q: So now, you are back in America, starting a new job. But the only religious figure in your life was Rabbi Shimoni.

A: Since my new job was in New York, and Rabbi Shimoni was in New Jersey, my weekly visits with him naturally came to an end. He had invested a tremendous amount of time and energy in me. Years later, he admitted to me that he was concerned that without his continued guidance and influence my interest in Judaism might wither. However, *Hakadosh Baruch Hu* has many messengers, and *hashgacha pratis* still would not give me any peace.

A few weeks after I started working at the Sperry Corporation, I found myself sharing a room with Nathan Ziv, who was very religious. We were the only two people in the room, and entire days could go by without us having much contact with anyone else, so we quickly became quite friendly. Years later, his wife, Dina, told me that he had come home one day and told her, "We have a new nice young guy at work. I think he's Jewish, but I'm really not sure."

A few months went by. One day, Nathan and I were walking to the computer room, and I decided to surprise him. I asked him a question in Hebrew. He almost dropped to the floor.

"What! You speak Hebrew?" he asked in astonishment.

"Yes," I smiled. "I've been going to an *ulpan* for a number of years."

"Well," he said, "if you know Hebrew, then we should be learning *mishnayos* together at lunchtime."

Q: Did you know what he was talking about?

A: Not really. He explained to me what they were, and so we started to learn together. He also invited me to join him at the Mincha minyan at work, but that was a bit too much for me, and I didn't go. As time went on, and we became more and more friendly, he asked me if I would like to join him and his family for Shabbos. On the one hand, I wanted to accept his invitation, but on the other hand, I was afraid. I knew that if I were to go, I wouldn't be able to leave; I would be imprisoned until Shabbos was over. I politely resisted his repeated invitations.

Another development at this point in my life when I started working at Sperry was that I saw a lot more of my grandparents, since I passed their apartment on my way home from work.

Q: Did you tell your grandparents about your new friends and your interest in Judaism?

A: They knew I was interested in Judaism, but they didn't know how serious I was. I did not make a big deal of it, because I knew that the relationship between my mother and her parents was very delicate, and I didn't want to say something that might harm it. I think my grandmother sensed that something was up. She used to say to me, "I know that you will marry a Jew. You would never marry a goy." They also knew I was learning Hebrew, because I would go over some words with my grandfather. There is a story I remember hearing: When we were little, my grandmother said about me, "You'll see. This one is mine. He's coming back to me."

One day, my grandmother told me that my aunt had decided to make them a party for their sixtieth wedding anniversary.

"I thought you were waiting for your seventy-fifth till you would have another party," I said.

I reminded her that when my parents, aunts and uncles had made them a very big party for their fiftieth wedding anniversary, at the end of the evening, the owner of the hall said, "We'll see you at your sixtieth anniversary!"

"No," my grandmother said, "my children paid a lot of money for this. You won't be seeing us till our seventy-fifth anniversary!"

As the date of their sixtieth wedding anniversary approached, two things appeared to be worrying my grandmother.

I had bought her and my grandfather tickets to a Yiddish play. They both spoke Yiddish, and in fact my grandmother's mother, my great-grandmother, had been an actress in Thomashefsky's Yiddish Theater in New York before she was married. I thought my grandparents would love the idea of going to a Yiddish play, but my grandmother kept asking me if I would be able to get the money back if they were unable to go.

"Nonsense," I would tell her. "Why wouldn't you be able to go?"

"Well, you never know, something might come up," she said. "Could you get the money back?"

I could not understand what she was worried about.

Her other cause for worry was the party. My aunt had invited my grandmother's brother and sister to the party. Over the years, she had very little contact with her brother and sister, in part because she had never told them about my mother's conversion, and she was horrified at the thought of their finding out. She had kept this secret for many years, and now it looked like the cat was about to come out of the bag.

"Do you think I can ask your mother not to wear her necklace with the cross?" my grandmother anxiously asked me.

My mother had been suffering from serious health problems. The relationship between her and her mother over the years had grown from total loss of contact to the point where they spoke almost daily on the telephone. Yet, there were still lines that were not crossed.

On the one hand, my grandmother would be embarrassed should her siblings find out about my mother's conversion. On the other hand, she did not want to hurt my mother.

"Listen," I told her, "I very much doubt that my mother would wear a cross to the party. Leave it be. If you open up a discussion, who knows where it might lead? My feeling is, don't say anything."

"Yes," she told me, "that's what your grandfather said. I won't say anything. You know, I realize that I was wrong to blame your mother all these years. It's really my fault. I didn't give her a Jewish education, so what could I have expected from her?"

Q: That was pretty harsh wasn't it? Don't you think your grandmother was being pretty hard on herself?

A: That was how she felt. She was at the end of her life. I think she was trying to make sense of things.

Q: She felt she was close to the end?

A: Although she was healthy and active, it seems that she did. After we finished discussing the necklace, she started to tell me stories about when she was young. Not just the usual ones I had heard millions of times. She told me stories she had never mentioned before — anecdotes, things from the past. She started to tell me more and more stories, as if she couldn't get them out fast enough. It was as if she knew this would be her last opportunity. It was getting late, and I got up to leave. If only I had known that this was the end.

"Give me one ring when you get home," she reminded me at the door.

Whenever one of us visited, she would ask us to call her to let her know we had arrived home safely.

"Yes, Grandma. I'll ring you," I said.

"If we can't go to the show, will you be able to get the money back?"

"Good-bye, Grandma," I said sternly. "See you next week at the party!"

"We'll see," she said.

That was Thursday; on Sunday she was dead.

Monday morning was stormy — rain, clouds, thunder — and for a brief moment the clouds broke and there was a rainbow. I saw it and felt connected with my grandmother; it was her ring saying, "I'm home safely." It would be many years before I would learn that we make a blessing upon seeing a rainbow.

Q: You really miss her, don't you?

A: Yes, I miss her and my grandfather dreadfully. It's been nearly twenty years since she passed away and ten since my grandfather's passing. The pain of the loss is less frequent, but not any less severe.

The funeral took place Monday afternoon. And

now, listen to this: my older brother, the Baptist minister, came in for the funeral. He was wearing his suit and jacket. We were just about to leave our apartment when my mother noticed that he was wearing a pin with a cross on it.

"Roger," she said, "take that pin off!"

"Why?" he asked.

"Because," she said, "you are going to your grandmother's funeral, and she wouldn't want you going with that pin. Out of respect for your grandmother, take it off!"

"I am not ashamed of what I am," he protested.

"I am also not ashamed of what I am," she replied, "but out of respect for your grandmother, either you take it off or don't go with us!"

I imagined myself saying to my grandmother, "Grandma! Why were you so worried about that necklace?"

Q: Did your brother take off the pin?

A: You bet he took it off. He saw that my mother wasn't going to take no for an answer.

Q: I am sure you keep your grandmother's *yahrtzeit*, but does your mother?

A: As a matter of fact, my mother lights a *yahrtzeit* candle for both her parents. I call her every year to remind her of the dates, and she is very faithful to light a candle in their memory.

Q: What about those tickets?

A: Well, my grandmother was right all along. I couldn't get the money back for those tickets. I certainly wasn't going to give them to my grandfather, and I wasn't going to go. I gave them to Nathan, my religious friend at work. His wife, Dina, and one of his daughters went to the play.

Dina called me up a few days later to thank me for the tickets, "I'm sorry about the circumstances." she told me. "The children really would like to meet you. Purim is coming up. Will you join us for the festive Purim meal? It's not like Shabbos. If you see that we are going to bite you, you can leave."

I thought about it for a moment and said, "Okay. I'm looking forward to it."

5

" PURIM "

Q: So you went to the Ziv's for Purim?

A: Yes. I had no idea what to expect. I certainly didn't expect to see adults dressed up in costumes. The house was crowded because when the Zs (a.k.a. Zivs) do something, they do it in a very big way.

There were three or four tables set up in the living and dining rooms, and they must have had about thirty to forty guests for their Purim *seuda*. I must admit that I felt a little bit funny because, apart from Nathan, I didn't know anyone there. He was busy running back and forth, fetching and carrying, following Dina's orders to the best of his ability, and greeting his guests. Finally, they said it was time to wash. I didn't know what they meant, but I went to the kitchen with everyone else and stood on line in front of the sink. I saw that everyone took a strange-looking container with two handles, filled it with water and poured it over their hands. I thought this a rather odd custom, but when in Rome... I did the same. After that, they motioned me to sit next to Nathan's thirteen-year-old middle son, Aaron.

It took quite some time for everyone to have his turn at the sink, so I thought I would take the opportunity to get acquainted with Aaron until everyone was seated.

I turned to him and said, "What's your name?"

"Ugh, ugh," he grunted while making the strangest hand gestures, putting one hand above the other, and rotating his wrist a couple of times. He then reversed the positions of his hands and rotated the other wrist.

I presumed he must have developmental problems, and, because I did not want him to feel badly, I repeated my question slowly and in a loud voice, in the hopes I could make myself better understood.

"WHAT...IS...YOUR...NAME?"

He continued to grunt, but I was not deterred.

"WHERE…DO…YOU…GO…TO…SCHOOL?" I inquired.

"Ugh, ugh," he repeated again, wildly moving his hands, touching his mouth, and pointing at the bread on the table.

Gee, it's really sad, I thought. *His father is an accomplished computer programmer, very intelligent, and his poor son…*

I sat there with an uncomfortable feeling, not knowing exactly what to do or say next. Finally, everyone had washed; Nathan made the blessing on the bread, and Aaron turned to me and in a clear, normal voice told me his name and where he went to school. Now it was my turn to be dumbfounded. He explained that according to Jewish law, we wash our hands before eating bread, and that it is prohibited to talk between the washing and the blessing.

Now, that's an interesting practice, I thought.

A few years later, when Aaron made a *siyum* on *Shas*, I reminded him of my first impression and told him with a smile, "It's amazing how much you've progressed since you've known me!"

This story has been retold countless times in the Z family. We still laugh about it today. That Purim was an amazing experience for me. I thought Orthodox Jews were always very serious. I never realized they could have so much fun.

Soon after this memorable experience, the Zs decided to see if I was brave enough to accept a Shabbos invitation. I had wanted to go for a long time, but I was nervous. My Purim visit broke the ice, and now I felt comfortable enough to accept. This was Dina's plan, and of course it worked.

Not long after this Purim at the Z's, I started attending adult education courses at Lincoln Square Synagogue. I wanted to know more about Judaism. The first course I took was an introductory course in *Chumash*. I was disappointed, though, since the material did not go much beyond the basic narrative already familiar to me.

The following semester I took an intermediate course in *Chumash*, and it was great. During this course we were exposed to the great commentators — I can safely say that I had not come across them as a child — Rashi, Ramban, and Ibn Ezra.

The rabbi who taught the course, Rabbi Yossi Weiser, was very dynamic. I became quite close to him. Whenever I saw that he was teaching a course, I enrolled. In addition to his *Chumash* courses, he also taught several courses in *mussar*, using Rabbi Dessler's *Michtav Me'Eliyahu*.

Lincoln Square created an intellectual environment that was crucial to my further development. As I joined the Zs for more and more Shabbatot, I became closer and closer to them. They provided the warm emotional environment necessary for me to take my next steps.

Q: So now you were able to go full-steam ahead. You had a place to go to for Shabbos, and you had a regular learning schedule. In other words, things were really moving along, weren't they?

A: Yes, and I received another boost when I made an unplanned trip to Israel. This was my third visit to the country.

Q: Your third visit!? You never told us about the second visit!

A: Well, that trip did not have a major effect on me. It was the spring of 1985, and I went with my younger sister. I was so busy showing her the sights and making sure she had a good time, it was not practical for me to leave her alone to attend classes in a yeshiva, which perhaps I would have done had I been on my own. As it was, an Arab offered to buy her from me.

Q: Surely you're joking. Aren't you?

A: Believe me, I'm not. In fact, to this day she claims I was out to sell her. You see, her dream in going to Israel was to ride a camel. Why on earth she just didn't go to the Bronx Zoo is beyond my understanding! It certainly would have been much cheaper. In any event, we went up to the Intercontinental Hotel on the Mount of Olives, where Arabs wait for tourists wanting camel rides.

Laurie is afraid of heights, and when the camel stood up, she let out a bloodcurdling scream that was probably heard all over Jerusalem. The Arab whose camel she was on must have found her scream enchanting, because he asked me if she was my wife. When I laughed and said, "No, she's my sister," he immediately said, "How much do you want for her?"

I was pretty shocked by the offer. Then I thought of all the wealth Avraham received because of Sarah, and briefly considered it. In the end, though, I told him that my parents would probably ask questions if I returned to the States without her.

Later in the day, my sister sent a picture postcard to our parents with the message, "Today, your son tried to sell me for two camels and a goat. Really wish you were here. With love, Laurie."

In the fall of 1985, my company went out on strike. You have no idea what *hashgacha* this was.

I had a good friend, not religious, who had learned with me in the *ulpan*. Walter had made aliya a few years before and was having a very difficult time in Israel. He was single, and very lonely. We spoke on the telephone quite often, and I tried to encourage him. (He is now living in the States, and he and his wife are just wonderful people. Of my close friends from my pre-*teshuva* days, only Walter remains. It's unbelievable how encouraging they were to me as I made my way back to Judaism, especially when you consider the fact that they are not observant.) As I said, he was having a hard time. I phoned him to tell him about the strike.

He said, "Maybe you could use the opportunity to come to Israel now. I could really use a friend."

"Well," I told him, "the strike may end at any time. I don't think it makes sense to come if I may just have to return right away."

After hanging up the phone, I thought, *Well, why can't I go? Why should I stay here manning the picket line when I could be in Israel?*

I was still living with my parents, and I had very few financial obligations, so I called my boss, Lou. When I told Lou what I wanted, he said, "Heck, this &*!@% thing is going to go on for a long time. Go for it!"

And so here I was on my way to Israel for the third time.

I left the States during *chol hamoed Sukkos*. I had been staying with the Zs for the first days of Sukkos, and they were very excited for me. They told me how wonderful Simchas Torah is in Eretz Yisrael. I was very excited too. But guess what? I missed it! My calendar, printed in America, was meant for the Diaspora. It listed Simchas Torah as being the day after Sukkos is over in Eretz Yisrael. You see how my knowledge of the most basic things in Judaism was lacking.

Anyway, on this trip, I was much more receptive to the spiritual forces of Eretz Yisrael than I had been on my previous visits. My nervousness about accepting Shabbos invitations had vanished. The courses at Lincoln Square were exposing me to Jewish concepts. I was keeping my "modified kosher," and I was also keeping a "modified Shabbos." I tried to avoid writing on Shabbos, except for my Hebrew homework (because, of course, this was holy). In short, I had moved far enough along to see things with a somewhat different set of eyes.

So, here I was in Jerusalem. Naturally, I went to the *Kotel*, where a fellow came up to me and said, "Hi!" He handed me his card and asked, "How are you doing?" I glanced at it and saw his name was Jeffrey Seidel. (He is now running Heritage House in the Old City.)

I guess he wasn't quite sure what to make of me. I was wearing a cap, not a *kippa*.

"Have you ever spent a Shabbos with a religious family?" he inquired.

"Yes," I told him. "In America I have some friends who I go to from time to time."

"Well," he said, "Shabbos in Jerusalem is really special. Would you like me to arrange a Shabbos meal for you?"

"Thank you," I said, "I would like that very much."

"I'll be waiting for you here at the fountain Friday night."

So, on Friday night, I returned to the *Kotel*.

I really enjoyed seeing the people coming down to the Wall, singing and dancing. I made my way to the fountain, where Jeffrey was standing with a small group of people. He introduced me to my hosts. Together with their other guests, I walked with them to their apartment in the German Colony.

We had a lovely time. There was lots of singing, interspersed with lively conversation. The meal was delicious, and my host said over some interesting *divrei Torah*.

By now it was getting late. I heard thunder in the distance.

"I have quite a walk back to my hotel," I told my host. "If you don't mind, I think I had better get going. It sounds like it might rain."

He said, "It wouldn't surprise me at all. We have

just started praying for rain!"

I was almost at the hotel when a gentle rain started.

"Look at that," I said to myself. "It really works!"

Jeff had asked me if I would like to go to a yeshiva on Sunday morning, "just to see what it is like." I agreed. He told me to be at the *Kotel* on Sunday morning. "Rabbi Meyer Shuster will take you to the yeshiva along with a group of other young men."

Saturday morning, my friend Walter and his future wife, Vered, joined me for a stroll in the Old City. All of a sudden, a bunch of religious kids jumped in front of our path, and one of them said to me, "Remember, you're supposed to meet my father tomorrow at the *Kotel*!"

At first I had no idea who they were or how they knew me. After a few moments, I realized that they must be Rabbi Shuster's children. They must have been at the *Kotel* when I was speaking to Jeff Seidel, but I hadn't noticed them at the time.

Anyway, on Sunday morning Rabbi Shuster piled us into his station wagon and took us to Yeshiva Ohr Sameach. Little did I realize that eight years later I would be living in Jerusalem near the yeshiva, and learning there at nights with my *chavrusa*, study partner!

I sat in on a few courses. I especially enjoyed

Rabbi Gottlieb's lecture concerning Jews and liberalism.

I also sat in on an *ulpan* offered by the yeshiva. I was not particularly impressed. The teacher, incredibly enough, was not a native Israeli and didn't seem to know the language very well. I thought to myself, *In all of Israel they couldn't find someone who is able to teach the language properly?*

I am very grateful for having had the opportunity to learn Hebrew in a professional manner. The first time I picked up a siddur to daven, I understood what I was saying. I can pick up a Hebrew *sefer*, read it and understand it better than many students who have spent years learning full-time.

I think it's absolutely crazy that *baalei teshuva* should skip over acquiring this basic skill. I am convinced that by investing time in learning the language properly, the dividends would be well worth it, and everything else would become much easier.

Q: This obviously bothers you very much.

A: Yes, it bothers me a great deal. When I was living near Ohr Sameach, I spoke with many *baalei teshuva*, and you have no idea of the feelings of inferiority and frustration engendered because of the deficiency in basic Hebrew-reading skills. If a Jew can't pick up a Hebrew *sefer* and understand it, he will never feel truly at home in the Orthodox world. I think that people tend to forget that most *baalei teshuva* will not remain in yeshiva for years and years. If they are not given the basic tools — such as Hebrew and a solid foundation in *Chumash* — they will lack the skills necessary to become committed *baalei batim* later in life, and will never reach their true potential.

Q: You haven't said anything about the spiritual aspects of this visit to Israel. Did it affect you in any way, or was it more of an intellectual journey?

A: Well, a few weeks after I returned to America, I became somewhat depressed. With each passing day, my depression got deeper, and at first, I didn't understand why. One day it hit me: I didn't feel at home. I said to myself, "This is crazy. Here is this little country, Israel, that I have been to only three times — each visit lasting not more than a few weeks — yet I feel it is mine. On the other hand, America, where I was born and grew up, feels so alien to me."

I felt as if I no longer belonged. In contrast, I felt so connected to the land of Israel. I noticed small changes that had taken place in Israel since my previous visit: a new road, a new footbridge, a new neighborhood. The amazing thing was that I felt they were mine. They belonged to me. I felt my whole mind-set changing.

In addition to my increasing connection to the land of Israel, I felt the need to be more connected to Jewish observance — and yet, at the same time, I felt very uneasy about this. I was being pulled along against my will, and I didn't like it; I was no longer in control. Whenever I took on a new observance, I immediately thought, "Well, if you are doing this, then now it doesn't make sense if you don't do that." For instance, I realized that if I wasn't going to write on Shabbos, that included not even doing my Hebrew homework, although in my eyes, it was holy. I began to do more and more, davening more, wearing tzitzit, sometimes willingly, sometimes less so.

Q: Did your family notice the change in you?

A: No. They didn't say anything. It is strange though, because for me a whole new world was coming into existence. I remember that soon after I got back from Israel, I spent a Shabbos with the Zivs. Our company was still on strike, and negotiations had been resumed. Before Shabbos, I wondered how the weekend negotiations would turn out. Both sides had a recorded message to update the workers about the status of the negotiations, but Nathan and I would have to wait until after Shabbos to call.

After Shabbos ended, we cleaned up, and talked for a while. We had a late *melave malka* and suddenly I remembered.

"We have to phone to find out if we are working on Monday!" I exclaimed.

I had completely forgotten about work and the strike. Shabbos had taken me into a completely different world. I suddenly became aware of the possibility of living in a sort of parallel world where "reality" was suspended and I was connected to G-d, Shabbos and the *chagim*.

6

 **Shabbos**

Q: What was your next step?

A: Thanks to the adult courses in Judaism at the Lincoln Square Synagogue, I also became much more aware of the role of the Jewish people in history. In our *Chumash* class, we discussed the faith of Avraham, and his willingness to sacrifice his son.

We discussed those Jews in Spain who willingly gave up their lives for Judaism rather than submit to Christianity. Their deaths were a real *kid-*

dush Hashem, sanctification of G-d's name. This was not a casual belief in G-d. When other Jews saw their sacrifice, they would have to understand that their love and belief in G-d transcended everything, even life itself. I was told that the Jews who were murdered during the Shoah also died *al kiddush Hashem*, but I had difficulty accepting this because those Jews did not have a choice; the Germans took it away from them. They were not even killed because of who they were, but rather because of who their grandparents were, and it had absolutely nothing to do with their beliefs or level of observance. Therefore, I found it difficult to understand how their deaths could sanctify Hashem's name.

I pondered this issue for many months, and I finally understood that as long as we live as Torah-observant Jews, then other Jews will look at us and see that despite the enormous price that has been paid, there are nevertheless Jews who remain loyal to Hashem and His commandments, and perhaps this will inspire them to lead a Torah-observant life.

This brought me to a frightening conclusion. I would in a sense be robbing those Jews of the meaning of their sacrifice unless I chose to live as an observant Jew. I understood that I simply had to do more.

It was the summer of 1986, the Fourth of July

weekend. I started to keep Shabbos. I guess you might call it my Independence Day!

Q: The Zivs must have been thrilled!

A: Actually, I didn't tell them because I thought that if I failed, it would be worse than not doing anything at all, which would in fact bring about a *chilul Hashem*, rather than the *kiddush Hashem* I was looking for. I was especially concerned about having to leave work early on Fridays during the winter, so I resolved not to tell anyone that I was keeping Shabbos until the shortest Friday of the year. If I could get that far, then I knew everything would work out.

Q: And now the obvious question is: what about your family? You were still living at home, and you couldn't very well hide your Shabbos observance. How did you work things out at home?

A: It was a challenge. A real challenge. It was hard to capture the real atmosphere of Shabbos at home. The phone would be ringing, the television would be on, etcetera, etcetera.

Q: What about kashrus at home? Cooking? What did you eat on Shabbos?

A: During the week, I would do all my cooking in the microwave. I used disposable dishes, and double-wrapped everything. On Shabbos, I managed with cold food.

Q: Said like that, it doesn't sound so bad, but it must

have been very hard. The picture is one of you sitting all alone at one corner of the kitchen table.

A: There was most definitely a sense of loneliness. I was becoming disconnected from my old world while the connections to my new world were only just starting to develop. I had the restrictions of Shabbos, but I didn't have the *kedusha*, the holiness of Shabbos. I would often go to the Z's to feel the warmth of Shabbos. It was difficult, but the difficulties were made easier to overcome by the realization that I was part of something larger than myself. Perhaps it sounds overly cosmic, but I felt that my role in this world was to restore a lost faith to our family. I intuitively understood that Shabbos was the key. If I failed to keep it properly, then all would be lost forever.

Q: By now your mother must have had quite a collection of gray hairs. Did she ever try to discourage you?

A: No, but she would sometimes shake her head in disbelief. When I told her that I was going to try and keep Shabbos properly, her only response was, "What next?!" but she never tried to stop me.

Q: Which is incredible really. What about your father? Was he supportive?

A: Not especially. But he also didn't come out against it. I would say he was indifferent. Occasionally he made fun of Jewish observance, saying, "What's the big deal if I turn on a light? Do you think G-d cares if I turn on a light just because it's Saturday?" When he made remarks like that, my mother would quiet him.

Q: It sounds like your mother was very respectful. Or was she just making the best of a situation where she saw that you had reached the point of no return?

A: My mother was very respectful and extremely considerate. For example, if she wanted to watch TV, she would do so in her own room because she knew I wouldn't sit in the living room with the TV on. She also tried very hard to remember not to switch off the bathroom light. Sometimes she would forget, and I would admonish her, saying, "Why can't you leave it on?"

"So I'll turn it back on for you," she'd say apologetically.

Before she could reach the switch, I would tell her, "Oh, never mind. It's too late. Just leave it alone."

At this, she would roll up her eyes, shake her head, and say to herself in exasperation, "I just don't understand what he wants from me."

7

"GOVERNORS ISLAND"

Q: Weren't there any other Jewish families who lived nearby to whom you could have gone for an authentic, spiritual Shabbos?

A: As I said, we lived on Governors Island, which was a Coast Guard base. My father was in the Coast Guard, and there was only a handful of Jews on the Island. Nevertheless, there was a synagogue which had served the many Jews drafted into the army when the Island had been an army base.

I found out that Shabbos services were held once

a month; there was not enough demand for anything beyond this.

I was curious and said to myself, "I think I'll go and see what it is like."

We didn't know any of the Jews who lived on the Island, and I hoped that maybe I would meet others who shared my interest in Judaism.

Unfortunately, it was not at all what I expected. They brought in a reform rabbi to conduct the services. There were very few people, and there was no davening.

Q: No davening? What did they do then?

A: Well, I am fairly certain that no one there had any familiarity with Jewish liturgy. Understanding this, the rabbi dispensed with the davening and proceeded to deliver a sermon. He quoted here and there from a siddur. For example, he read one of the morning *berachot*, blessings, and said, "People used to say this in the morning." He talked a bit about Shabbos, saying, "People used to refrain from..."

As he went on, the *shiur* got more "advanced." He started quoting from the Gemara, clearly taking things out of context, and even went as far as finding a source for justification of behavior deemed an abomination by the Torah. I may have known very little about Judaism, but I knew that something was wrong here.

Q: How did you know at this point that what he was saying had no basis in halacha? After all, you were still very much at the beginning of your journey back to Judaism.

A: I was familiar with the biblical text from when I was a child, and I knew that the Bible condemned certain behavior in no uncertain terms. Don't forget that I grew up in a fundamentalist church where the Bible was taken literally, so I already had deep suspicions if someone were to say something contrary to the text. I knew something was not kosher here!

After the service, they had a kiddush in a side room. Needless to say, I didn't eat a thing! The rabbi came over and introduced himself and asked me if I was new to Governors Island.

"No," I said, "I have been living here for some time. I am becoming more interested in Judaism, so I decided to come and see what you had to offer."

He said, "Well, we are glad you came. I hope you enjoyed yourself. By the way, what did you think of my sermon?"

"Frankly," I said, "it didn't make sense to me. You kept talking about what people used to do, but I have friends who are doing all these things right now. They go to shul — not just once a month, either — and they daven three times a day. They keep Shabbos, they eat kosher. So why do you keep saying, 'Jews used to'?"

He answered me, "Most Jews don't do these things anymore, but that doesn't mean that they are not Jews."

"But there are Jews who do keep the laws today. Maybe some of the people here don't even know that. I think that even if you don't keep the laws, you cannot ignore those Jews who do. And what is all this nonsense about Judaism sanctioning deviant behavior?"

"Ahhh," he said, "I can see that you have already fallen under the influence of the Orthodox, and I know what they say about me. The Orthodox Jews in my family don't even think I am a Jew."

"Is your mother Jewish?" I asked him.

"Of course she is! Why do you ask?"

"Well," I said, "then they know that you are a Jew. They just don't think you're a rabbi!"

Q: You actually said that to him?

A: Yes, I did. I said it without thinking. To tell you the truth, I still can't believe that came out of my mouth.

He was curious about me and started asking me about my background and how I became interested in Judaism. He was fascinated when I told him that my family had left Judaism to become Christians.

Q: Forgive me for interrupting you, but was this

before or after you told him that he wasn't a rabbi?

A: After.

Q: And he was still talking to you? He didn't throw you out of his shul?

A: No. He didn't seem to be offended. I guess he had heard worse from his family. I also think that he understood that I had no intention of insulting him. I was just stating a fact.

Anyway, he told me, "You know that we also do *kiruv* work in the Reform movement. I come to places like Governors Island, and I am also active on college campuses as well as other outreach programs to try and bring people closer to Judaism."

I said to him, "Would you do me a favor?"

"What do you have in mind?" he asked me.

"I know of people who were raised as Reform Jews who had reached a certain point where they were looking for something more meaningful. Ignorant of anything beyond Reform Judaism, they determined that there was no real meaning to be found in Judaism, and they adopted the Christian faith. If only they had known that Judaism does have more to offer! I hope that if in the future, you should ever come across a Jew who feels like this, you will have the honesty to admit that you do not represent all that the Jewish faith has to offer and direct him to an Orthodox rabbi."

While we were talking, one of the members of the rabbi's flock, a Jewish officer in the Coast Guard, interrupted and handed the rabbi a form saying, "You need to fill this out so that the Coast Guard can pay you."

The rabbi took a pen from his pocket, handed it to the officer, and said, "Would you mind filling it out for me? I don't write on Shabbat."

I was stunned. I never set foot in that place again.

Q: Did you confront him about it?

A: No, he was rushing to catch the next ferry.

Q: Well, that certainly takes care of the Reform movement, but what about the Conservatives? Did you ever have any contact with them?

A: When I was at the *ulpan*, I became friends with a very nice fellow, Binyamin, who was a very committed Conservative Jew. His father came from an Orthodox background, but, like many of his generation, he did not find his place in the Orthodox shuls that existed in the States in the first half of the twentieth century.

My grandfather had a similar story. He told me that the Orthodox synagogues were very small, not particularly clean, and very cliquish. They were filled with older people drinking schnapps, but there weren't very many young people to be found. The Young Israel movement got its start by trying to create an environment where young Jews would feel comfortable. Many Jews, however, like Binyamin's father and my grandfather, moved over to the Conservative movement.

Pesach was approaching, and everyone in my *ulpan* was discussing his or her plans for the seder nights.

"Where will you have the seder?" Binyamin asked me.

I told him, "I've never been to a seder."

So he said, "Well, then you'll come to ours!"

For the next five years, I joined his family for the seders.

They always had a beautiful seder. His aunts and uncles would come. He also had an Orthodox cousin who joined them before he got married. I got to know the family well over the years.

His father led the seder the first year I came. The following year, his father joined us for just parts of the seder. He could not sit for long periods. He was suffering terribly from cancer. Half his face was eaten away, and he had lost an eye. Not long afterward, he passed away. The next year the table seemed so empty without him. Binyamin married and moved out to eastern Long Island, near where his sister lived. His mother bought a place in the same town. One of the uncles had also passed away. Things were different, but nevertheless the seder was lovely. At this point, I was a few months away from becoming *shomer Shabbos*. The next morning, Binyamin told me that we would go to shul, but because it was so far, we would have to drive. We got into the car, and Binyamin said, "You have your *kippa* on. You need to take it off."

"Why should I take it off?" I asked.

"Because we are driving, and you're not allowed to drive on Pesach."

I was really confused. Binyamin was so knowledgeable about Judaism compared to me, and I really looked up to him, but I just didn't understand.

"So why are we driving?" I asked.

"Because the shul is very far. It's impossible to walk there. We're not living in Bayswater anymore."

"I don't know," I said. "If we're not supposed to drive, then how does it help to take our *kippot* off?"

"Will you just take it off?" he pleaded with me impatiently. "We are going to be late for shul!"

As we drove to shul he told me that he realized that driving on Pesach was a contradiction.

"But you know," he said, "everyone lives their lives

with all sorts of contradictions. The Orthodox also live with their contradictions."

"But don't you think we shouldn't just accept the contradictions but instead try to minimize them?"

"It's a personal matter. Everyone finds the level of contradictions with which he is comfortable. But let's stop this discussion. Here's the shul."

That was the last Pesach I spent with my good friend. Just before the following Pesach, his mother died of heart and kidney failure. When we returned to her house after the funeral, I saw her Pesach shopping list on the refrigerator door.

A few days later Binyamin called me. He said, "I would really appreciate it if you could join us for the seder. You are one of the few people left from the old days. My father is gone, my uncle passed away, and now my mother is gone. Please come."

I hesitated. By this point I was *shomer Shabbos*, but how could I refuse my dear friend Binyamin in such circumstances? Kashrut wasn't an issue; they kept to very high standards.

"Well, I don't know…"

"Please come."

"Okay, I'll come, but I can't drive to shul. I'll just stay at home."

"No," he said, "that won't work. We are having the

second seder at my sister's house, and it's too far to walk."

I said, "I really …"

"Don't say any more," he interrupted. "I shouldn't have asked you. I apologize. I just miss everyone so much, and having you at the seder is a reminder of the good times we all had together, but I guess all that is over."

This was a real *nisayon* for me. It was hard to refuse a friend in need. I was very lucky that my friend was Binyamin. He understood. To this day, I can't tell you how much I appreciate his family's hospitality and graciousness in introducing me to Pesach. I try to call him every Pesach to reminisce over those days and to wish him well.

8

"A Home for Shabbos"

Q: I imagine the first Shabbos you kept really must stand out in your mind. What was it like?

A: Well, I have to admit it was somewhat lacking in *kedusha*. I was probably the only *shomer-Shabbos* Jew on Governors Island; there were no *zemirot*, there was no going to shul and no real *seudos Shabbos*. Nevertheless, it was meaningful to me. Not only was it my first Shabbos, but I had to overcome what was for me a tremendous *nisayon*.

As I mentioned, it was the Fourth of July weekend in 1986. It was also the 100th anniversary of the Statue of Liberty, which is situated exactly opposite Governors Island. More than a year had gone into planning the celebration. President Reagan was slated to come to light the new torch of the statue using a laser beam from Governors Island. Many celebrities were to attend. It was to be a gala event, a real picture-taking opportunity. And I love to take pictures. I have been a photography buff since I was a young boy. When I realized that my first Shabbos would, of all weekends, be this weekend, I tried to convince myself that there would be no harm in putting it off. I said to myself, "Well, what's the difference if I start this week or next?" But I knew there was a big difference. I had made up my mind to keep Shabbos properly, and I had to see it through. I did enjoy observing the fireworks and watching the festivities, but I did not take a single picture.

Q: I believe that in one of our earlier conversations you referred to this Shabbos as your Independence Day.

A: Yes, it really was. This first Shabbos didn't come for free; I was compelled to give up something that meant a great deal to me. Nevertheless, Shabbos won out over the shutter! The picture had changed completely; my attitude toward mitzvot was developing. I knew I was on the way.

Meanwhile, summer turned to autumn, and the

weeks and months flew by. I continued to keep Shabbos. Occasionally, I would go to the Z's, but more often than not, I would stay home.

Q: When Shabbos started to come in earlier, how did you manage at work?

A: I would leave work early on Fridays, making up the time during the rest of the week. No one seemed to notice. I also was not yet wearing a *kippa* at work, so no one suspected a thing. I would wait until Nathan left, and I would leave a few minutes later. He had no idea I was keeping Shabbos. As I mentioned, I did not want him to know until I had successfully made it through the shortest Shabbos of the year.

However, a few days before this Shabbos, Lou, my boss, called an emergency departmental meeting. Nathan was not involved in this project, so he was not present. We were writing a proposal, and Lou was not pleased with how it was shaping up.

Now, Lou was a great boss, but subtlety was not his strongest point. "Listen, guys," he said. "This &*%# thing stinks. It's a piece of garbage. Anyone who would submit something like this should be put in jail. We're going to throw the whole freaking thing out and start from scratch, and I just don't care what it takes. We're going to work evenings and Saturday, and we're going to get this &*@# thing right and get it in on time.

"And," he added, glaring at us, "if anyone has a problem with this he better &*@# well speak up RIGHT NOW!"

So here it was — The Moment of Truth — precisely on the Shabbos that was to be followed by my springing my grand announcement.

"Uh, Lou," I said, meekly putting up my hand, "I have a problem with this."

With a bemused look, Lou turned to me. I was probably the last person from whom he would expect an objection. But Lou was Italian, and he grew up among Jews. I guess he had noticed my leaving early on Fridays, and he must have put two and two together.

He drew a deep breath and in mild exasperation said, "All right, we're all going to work evenings, and except for you, we are going to work on Saturday. If necessary, you will work on Sunday, and we're going to get this &*@# thing right and get it in on time. And if anyone has a problem with this, he better &*@# well speak up RIGHT NOW!"

I couldn't believe I had gotten off so easily. I had been dreading this moment for a long time. I knew that eventually there would be a conflict with work, although I certainly didn't expect that it would be this week. I was so nervous when I raised my hand to object, and in a moment, the situation was resolved. I said to myself, "That's it? It was so easy?"

Q: Did that make you believe a little bit more in Hashem and in His *hashgacha*?

A: No, that's not how I looked at it at the time. I was just relieved. But looking back, it certainly was *hashgacha* that I had a boss like Lou.

It was also a very important lesson for me, because I realized that it is very easy to conjure up fears that prevent one from advancing. Generally, they turn out to be totally unrelated to the reality of the situation at hand. Once these problems are overcome, we realize how silly our fears were, and how much time has been wasted with worry. I have had to repeat this lesson many times since, so I guess I haven't learned it as well as I should have; nevertheless, it is true. When you know that something is right, you just have to, as Lou would say, "Jump in and do the &*@# thing the way you're supposed to."

Anyway, the following Monday when Nathan came into the office, I said to him, "Guess what? I have some news for you. Since the Fourth of July weekend, I have been keeping Shabbos!"

"WHAT?" he said. "Good for you! But on Governors Island? From now on you are coming to us for Shabbos. If you are keeping Shabbos, it has to be a real Shabbos, with *zemirot*, davening, Shabbos meals, and Torah. Our home is your home, okay?"

The next Shabbos, I went to my new Shabbos home.

That Shabbos, Dina told me, "We're not going to invite you anymore. Family doesn't need an invitation. If you're not coming, call us so that we shouldn't worry. Otherwise, we expect you to spend Shabbos with us."

A small room upstairs became known as my room. Dina and Nathan's children became like members of my own family.

I have to tell you that my gratitude to this family and to Hashem for bringing me to it knows no bounds. It's not every *baal teshuva* who gets to "grow up" in an observant family.

9

"My "Yiddishe" Mama"

Q: From everything you have been telling me, and despite her continued ties to Christianity, and maybe even her resistance to Judaism, I still get the feeling that your mother is proud of you, very proud of you for having the courage and the tenacity of purpose to go against everything you were taught at home for so many years. I think that in her heart of hearts, she knows you are right and perhaps wishes that she too had the courage to do *teshuva*.

A: I cannot say what is in another person's heart of

hearts; however, I can make certain conclusions from what a person does, and I am convinced that despite everything, my mother retains, in a certain sense, a very strong Jewish self-identity. As I mentioned, although my mother was worried as my identification with Judaism increased, and although she would have preferred that it had been otherwise, hers was not an active opposition. You also remember how she ordered my older brother to remove his lapel pin with a cross before he went to my grandmother's funeral.

I will never forget when my older brother and his wife adopted their first child. The phone rang, and it was my mother.

"Bennie," she said, "I don't know if I should tell you this, because you're going to be very upset."

"Tell me what?" I asked.

"Never mind. I'm sorry I brought it up in the first place. I don't want to upset you."

"Tell me," I insisted. "What happened?"

"Well, all right, I'll tell you. Your brother and sister-in-law are not going to have the baby circumcised."

"So what?" I replied.

"You're not upset?" she asked incredulously.

"Of course I'm not upset. The baby isn't Jewish. What does he need to be circumcised for?"

"You're really not upset?" she repeated.

"No. Are you upset?" I asked.

"Of course I'm upset!" she said.

"Why are you so upset?" I asked. "Don't tell me it bothers you to have an uncircumcised grandson?"

"Oh, never mind," she said in an annoyed voice. "I should have known better than to tell you."

On another occasion, my mother put me in my place. My grandfather had a siddur, a prayer book, which had belonged to his father. On several occasions, he wanted to give it to me. I told him, "Grandpa, if you've kept it all these years, it must mean a lot to you, so keep it."

Once, my brother came to visit, and he picked up the siddur and admired it.

"Oh, you like it?" my grandfather said, "Take it; it's yours."

"Thanks," my brother said, and he took the siddur.

I was very upset when I found out about this. My brother kept the siddur displayed on a shelf, next to some antique eyeglasses. I mentioned to my mother how upset I was, and she said something very revealing to me.

"Bennie," she said, "your whole way of life connects you to your grandfather — your friends, your synagogue, your holidays. Everything you do connects you to him. This is the only connection your brother has. Why should you begrudge him that?"

I dropped the subject. I knew she was right.

I will tell you another story that illustrates the fact that my mother is a very unusual person and definitely still has a Jewish *neshama*.

Mom had quit her college studies when she started to have children. When we were more or less grown up, my mother decided to return to school. She received her BA with honors and went on to a PhD program. Not long after she started, she became quite ill. For a while, she struggled on, not wanting to give up her studies. Eventually, two surgeries forced her to quit, and in fact she has been in extremely poor health ever since.

The following incident took place right after Jimmy Carter, then president, fired Andrew Young, the US Ambassador to the United Nations. Carter apparently had sent Young to meet with Arafat, and it caused a big uproar in the Jewish community. Carter disassociated himself from Young and fired him to placate the Jewish public. It caused a big scandal and engendered an outburst of anti-Semitism among many blacks. Andrew Young was the first black to be given a cabinet-level position, and now he was pushed out due to Jewish pressure.

My mother used to travel back and forth to school

using the subway even though every bump caused her tremendous pain. She was very sick and could hardly move. A black man came into the subway car in which she was traveling. He looked around the car, and his eyes rested on a young fellow, perhaps a high school kid or a young college student. He glared at him and growled, "I'm going to kill the Jews! What do you think you did to Andrew Young? You can't bear to see a black man get ahead. I'll show you!"

He started moving toward the young man, and the people sitting or standing near him started to move away, leaving him alone to face his tormentor.

My sick, timid mother was sitting at the opposite end of the car. She got up, dragged herself over to where the young man was sitting and sat down right next to him. She glared at the aggressive fellow as if to say, "You do anything to him, you'll have to deal with me first." And he backed down.

Q: That certainly took courage. I don't know how many people would have had that kind of courage; it certainly shows that she empathized with him. Do you think she did it because she felt a kinship with him, being a Jew, or would she have done this for anyone?

A: I don't know, but I think that standing with and protecting another Jew was definitely a factor. I saw this identification with Jews many years before when I was about nine or ten years old. My mother was the church Sunday school superintendent, and she dragged me along to some Christian convention. There was a workshop on how to "witness" to Jews, that is, how to do missionary work with them. The speaker instructed his listeners, "You have to be very careful when you are speaking to Jews. They are very crafty, and they will twist your words. They will try to confuse you, so you need to plan exactly what you want to say." He continued speaking like this, conjuring up all kinds of anti-Semitic stereotypes.

My mother was fidgeting in her seat, and getting more and more agitated. Finally, she stood up. She interrupted his speech. "Pastor So-and-so, I thought that Christianity was supposed to be about love, yet all I hear coming out of your mouth is hate. If you want to convince Jews, or anybody for that matter, why don't you try a little love?"

With that, she grabbed my hand and stormed out of the room. Quite a few people followed her out.

This took a tremendous amount of courage for my mother. She is a timid person and doesn't like to draw attention to herself. This is why this story and the subway story say a lot.

My mother is also a very honest person. The raison d'être of an Evangelical Christian is to convert people, and Jews are considered a very special prize. I remember that once we were at some high school event, and there was a member of our church, Willy, who had pulled a man over to the side and was "witnessing" to him.

"I am a Jew," the man protested. "I can't become a Christian."

Willy saw my mother and called her over. "Meet my friend," he said. "She came from a very religious Jewish home, and today she is a Christian!"

My mother was aghast. She knew that Willy knew this wasn't so.

She told the man, "I am a Christian, but I do not come from a religious home. I knew virtually nothing of Judaism while I was growing up."

Not everyone saw my mother's Jewish background as an asset. When she became the Sunday school superintendent, one man tried to stir up opposition, saying it was dangerous to have somebody in that position when "we cannot be sure she is one of us."

Q: What was that supposed to mean?

A: You know, that she comes from the "other side."

Q: Was this said in your mother's earshot?

A: Yes.

Q: Did this upset her?

A: Yes, but he was a nasty person, prone to getting into arguments with a lot of people, so I don't think she took it too much to heart as she would have otherwise.

I also remember her watching the UN debate on

television when the "Zionism is Racism" resolution was passed. She was very upset. I remember her saying, "Look at this. They are planning another Holocaust."

Q: All of these stories have left me really confused. Does your mother regard herself as a Christian, or as a Jew and a Christian, you know one of those Hebrew-Christian messianic Jews?

A: She sees herself as a Christian.

Q: And yet, her Jewish inner core seems to surface unexpectedly every now and then.

A: Yes, I agree with you. I suppose that if you were to ask my mother, she would deny this behavior is a result of her being Jewish. However, she was the one that moved over to the boy in the subway car; she was the one that stood up in a crowd to protest the spewing of anti-Semitic stereotypes. She refused to act deceptively even in the "higher cause" of witnessing to a Jew. She watched the UN debate in horror, a horror I am sure her friends did not share.

What my mother feels in her heart of hearts, only *Hakadosh Baruch Hu* knows, but I am certain that the Jewish soul is there, and as you say, it surfaces unexpectedly every now and again.

10

"Outreach Issues"

Q: You mentioned that your mother felt very badly about the broken relationship that had existed between her and her mother for many years, yet I don't see any guilt feelings expressed about her part in what happened to cause the rift between them.

A: No, I don't think she has any guilt feelings about what happened, and from her point of view I wouldn't have expected her to. There is a difference between feeling guilty and feeling badly. For instance, despite the fact that I have managed to maintain a good relationship with most of my family, on many points there is a tremendous feeling of alienation. There are so many things that we see from a different point of view. I feel badly that I am unable to share in their celebrations. For instance, some years ago, a cousin of mine got married to a Catholic boy. I could not attend the ceremony, because that is what halacha, Jewish law, requires. I felt badly, but I certainly did not feel guilty.

Q: Of course as a practicing Jew you have to follow the halacha. You cannot participate in their Christian or mixed Jewish-Christian celebrations. But what does this have to do with your mother's abandoning the religion of her forefathers without the slightest pangs of conscience?

A: Let me remind you that, unfortunately, my mother's self-identification as a Jew was virtually non-existent. She became a Christian, but it would be hard to say that she left Judaism. She knew so little that there was really nothing to leave.

Q: Well, she did feel Jewish enough to want a menora!

A: True. At that point, I think she felt such a spiritual void that she was like a person drowning, reaching out to grab onto anything. It was Chanuka time, and I guess she felt she needed to do something to save herself from feeling her life lacked purpose.

Q: Look, I must be very dense, but none of this makes very much sense to me. She brought a menora into the house. Only a Jew would do that, so why didn't she go further?

A: Let me try to explain it to you. My mother knew next to nothing about Judaism. She did know that at Chanuka time, Jews light a menora. She expected and hoped that this would somehow fill a spiritual need. But she knew nothing about Chanuka, so screwing in another bulb night after night did nothing for her. Absolutely nothing. There were no Jewish *kiruv*, outreach, organizations at the time. There was no one to turn to. So when a neighbor invited her to a church, it was like a lifeline to her. She felt that her spiritual needs were being met.

Q: Do you know how?

A: Do I know how?

Q: Yes, I hope you don't mind me asking the question, but as someone who has experienced this kind of life from the inside, how would you say these needs were met?

A: I don't mind you asking the question, but I left the church. Obviously it didn't meet *my* needs.

Q: But you were connected to Christianity before you did *teshuva*. Maybe you didn't believe any of it all along?

A: No. Today I find it incredible that I really did believe it.

When my mother was younger, she taught poor

illiterate black woman how to read. She saw that as part of her mission as a Christian — to help people. It made her feel good. It made her feel worth something.

Q: But Judaism also commands a Jew to help others. Why did she have to go to Christianity for these ideas?

A: Because she didn't find it in Judaism, not because it is not there, but because she didn't know where or how to look. We lived in a town where there were few Jews, and no religious Jews at all. There was no one to help her. However, there was her Christian friend, who was willing to show her. The church was very welcoming. They told her that she had become an "ambassador for G-d." She could help to make a better world.

Q: But don't you think that a lot of this could be classified as general morality that the civilized world observes anyway? Everyone, the majority of decent people, wants to do good.

A: Not everyone wants to do good, and a large portion of those in the non-Jewish world who do, view morality as stemming from Christianity. Only after I learned more about Judaism did I discover that all the moral, ethical and ennobling values so admired by the world come from us, not, as I was taught, from Christianity.

My mother, though, did not have this knowledge. She apparently felt that she had joined a group of people who were doing G-d's will, and it gave her a great deal of satisfaction. She felt she was part of something larger than herself.

Q: Frankly, I don't understand what it is that gives them so much satisfaction, because for me, Christianity is a totally empty and meaningless belief system.

A: Actually, according to the Rambam, Christianity has a role to play in history — for non-Jews. He says that it will serve as a stepping-stone, eventually bringing them to acknowledge the truth of Judaism, so they will already be accustomed to the ideas of G-d and morality when Mashiach comes. For me, the existence of G-d was never an issue. The divinity of the Torah was never in doubt. And so, the transition to becoming an observant Jew was much easier for me because I had already become accustomed to these concepts.

Q: Well, I hope you're not advocating this as an innovative approach to Jewish education.

A: Obviously, I would not recommend my childhood education to anyone. However, for me it did serve as a stepping-stone.

I alluded to another factor that attracts Jews to Christianity: a sense of belonging. I think this also attracted my mother. Any convert, especially a Jewish convert, is welcomed with open arms.

I wonder if we can't improve on the welcome *we*

give newcomers. A *baal teshuva*, and all the more so a convert, is sometimes viewed with suspicion and may even, at times, feel unwelcome.

In America, there are a lot of Christian groups active on college campuses. They target Jews who are lonely, who feel they are missing something in life. We talk so much about antimissionary work, but I think that we devote far too little resources to pro-Judaism work. The missionaries tell them, "We care about you!" But we need to do more to show that we, their fellow Jews, care about them.

Q: But the missionaries don't really care about them. They care about snatching souls. They don't care about them the way we do. How can you say such a thing?

A: Maybe we need to care more. It's much more difficult to do what we should be doing, that is, reaching out to these Jews, than to blame the Christians and label them as soul-snatching monsters.

Q: But they *are* "soul-snatching monsters." They know that what they are doing to the Jew is wrong.

A: From their point of view, they don't believe they are doing something wrong. If they succeed in attracting a Jew away from his faith, then maybe we are at least partially to blame.

Q: You're blaming the victim! In other words, are you telling me that if I rob a bank, it's the bank's fault for being robbed?

A: If the guard responsible leaves his post at night, with the door open and the safe unlocked, then yes, it's the bank's fault if it's robbed! If we are the guardians of the Torah, and if we don't do our job, do you expect the missionaries to respect our heritage?

Q: Do you agree that any success they may have is because Christianity is less demanding than Judaism? I can almost guarantee that if you were to walk up to a secular Jew in the street today and talk about G-d or Judaism, you would be told "Get lost! I know all about Judaism. I am happy the way I am. Leave me alone!" But when the missionary approaches him, the Jew is flattered, perhaps because subconsciously he wants to be accepted by the non-Jewish world.

A: I really don't think this is true for the Jew who is searching. If he is attracted to Christianity, it's only because there is a Christian beside him welcoming him into the fold. If there was a Jew on the other side welcoming him into Judaism, with all its obligations, so long as it was done with love, I am convinced that his Jewish *neshama* would win out. The Christian succeeds only when the Jew isn't there and the loving Christian is.

Q: You mean to tell me that they are doing this because they love us? I believe that they are proselytizing us because they really hate us.

A: Listen, I think that whether they love or hate us

is immaterial. If they are proselytizing us because of love, it is just as dangerous or maybe even more so than if they are destroying us with hate. My main point is that we can't change the way they think, but we can and must change the way we relate to the unaffiliated Jew. If he knows that we care about him, then the battle is already well on its way to being won. The best way, the only way, to counteract Christian outreach is with Jewish outreach.

I think it is just terrible that there is so little in the way of an organized religious Jewish presence on the college campuses in America. When I was living in the States, I helped out a bit with one of the few such organizations that with precious little resources managed to do a lot on the few campuses where it was able to establish a presence. These groups could be doing much more, but it is so hard to raise money. Nevertheless, the Christian groups seem to have no problem making their presence felt everywhere.

Q: Because they have all the money. You have to ask yourself how many non-Jews there are in America compared to Jews. There are over two hundred million people in America, with only about five million Jews. So?

A: Blaming others is not what Judaism teaches. We have to try to figure out what we can do. You are right that in theory they have more resources available than we do, but it is a fact that Jews donate to all sorts of causes far and above others.

But what are we giving to? We have to examine ourselves and our priorities.

The last time I was in America, I visited a synagogue in a very wealthy area. The congregation has expanded this building many times over. When you step into the sanctuary, you sink a couple of inches into the carpet. The place looks like a theater. Our priorities are skewed.

And money also isn't the whole story. It doesn't cost a cent to make someone feel welcome. When my mother joined the church, she was welcomed with open arms. If she had any doubts, they melted in the warmth of the reception she was given.

On the other hand, the *baal teshuva* is not always warmly received. Many times he feels that he has come into a world where he is kept at arm's length.

Q: Why do you think he is kept at arm's length?

A: He's different. People are uncomfortable with people who are different. The *baal teshuva* has done a lot of soul-searching; he has questioned his values and lifestyle, and has made major changes in his life. Most people are content to remain wherever they are.

I think that it is similar to what the Gemara says about converts, that they are hard for the Jewish people. In the same way, the *baal teshuva* presents a challenge to the *frum* person.

I think there is another reason as well.

Christianity is an outreach religion; Judaism is not. For at least two thousand years, we have been "circling the wagons," trying to preserve what we have. Before the Enlightenment, almost all Jews were observant.

Q: The shtetl preserved them; the ghetto protected them from outside influences.

A: Yes, the rare Jew who left the community was seen as a traitor. There was no need to do outreach among Jews. Today the situation is very different. Most Jews today know nothing of Judaism. They may have not had anyone in the family who was observant for several generations. They have not betrayed anything or anyone. This requires a different response on the part of the *frum* community. We must adjust to this new reality and become more adept at outreach.

Q: Now wait a minute. I can't absolve the nonobservant Jew as easily as you do. Today we have an information media that makes nonsense of what you are saying.

A: Today we have an information media that makes nonsense out of everything.

Q: Maybe, but no Jew today can claim ignorance when it comes to keeping Shabbat or keeping kashrut. Radio, television, movies, newspapers, and the Internet bring an awareness of Judaism, if through nothing else than highlighting the tension between the religious and secular communities in

Israel. Everyone is aware of the issues at stake.

A: I disagree. The kind of exposure you are talking about does not bring knowledge of Judaism to the masses, but rather holds it up to ridicule. The image portrayed in the media is accepted as fact by most Jews who are not closely acquainted with anyone who is *frum*. We cannot blame the secular Jew. Instead, we need to change our mindset.

Q: To what effect?

A: To ensure that the *baal teshuva* does not feel that he is viewed with suspicion.

Q: Well, I'm not convinced that your criticism is valid. I never felt that I was viewed with suspicion, but I can understand and even justify the suspicion that may be felt by some *frum* Jews or even by the *frum* community at large. People make tremendous efforts to limit the outside influences on the home, to maintain an environment of *kedusha*, sanctity. Surely you would agree that the *baal teshuva*, given his background and exposure to non-Torah thought and influences, might sometimes represent a danger. After all, there are children, teenagers in the house. You have to protect them.

A: I think that people have to use common sense and always keep their eyes and ears open. A parent must be careful about what his child sees and hears even in a completely *chareidi* environment. I see this with my own children who attend *chareidi* institutions. But to say that a BT, because he is a BT, represents any more danger to the home than someone who is *frum* from birth (FFB), seems to me ridiculous.

I'm not only talking about Jews who are making their first steps into Judaism; I'm also talking about Jews who have been 100 percent *frum* for years. It's a well-known phenomenon that 100 percent acceptance is withheld. I find it very hard to believe that you are unaware of it and have not experienced it yourself.

Q: No, I must admit that I never did. Never! Not once!

A: I find that hard to believe. Maybe you just didn't notice it. Perhaps because you became *frum* at a later stage in life and probably had a much better sense of self and more self-confidence than the younger BT. But speaking for myself, and I have heard the same from many friends of my age who went through this experience, I can tell you that it can be very painful and very difficult to become a BT in the Jewish world as it is today. It needn't be that way. We have to change that. We need more sensitivity.

Q: You talk about difficulties. What was the most difficult thing?

A: The most difficult thing is the feeling of not being accepted.

I remember an article that made a stir some years

ago in one of the secular establishment Jewish newspapers. Now, this newspaper never had a good thing to say about the *frum* community and never had much credibility in religious circles. But one week they had an article about BTs in which the claim was made that most become disillusioned and return to a secular life. I remember one man saying, "You see how careful one needs to be? You just never know how serious they are!" It didn't matter that nothing in the article was backed up by facts or statistics. I would have hoped to hear at least one person express enough concern to ask, "What can we do to prevent disillusionment among *baalei teshuva*?"

Help with *shidduchim* is another area that needs improvement. Most often, the *baal teshuva* will be set up only with other BTs.

Q: Is that so terrible? People who get married generally come from similar backgrounds. There are enough BTs around to marry BTs. It's not as if there is a lack of them, both men and women. Why difference does it make if they marry fellow BTs?

A: It wouldn't make a difference, except for the message behind it. When I was looking for a *shidduch*, most suggestions were for women who were BTs. But there was another group that was drawn from as well.

Q: Which one?

A: I was considered a suitable candidate for FFB women who had been married before, women with children, women with medical problems or from families with medical problems. I was set up with a few women who had been married for only a few days. Let me be clear: they were fine women. There was not necessarily anything wrong with them. However, they did share something in common with the BTs: the *frum* community saw both groups as having problems. Even though people from the two groups had no common background, they were seen as being a possible match.

However, these norms are occasionally broken. I have a friend, a *ger*, convert, and we were once comparing our painful dating experiences. I mentioned to him that as a *ger*, he probably had a harder time than I did. He agreed, but added, "I may have had an easier time than most, though, because my profession is highly respected."

Q: Today, seventeen years down the line, do you still feel that you are not accepted? Left out? On the fringe? On the outside looking in?

A: Generally speaking, no. I have become integrated well enough that people are genuinely surprised when they learn I am a *baal teshuva*. This surprise also says a lot. But on a deeper level, I still feel I am not completely accepted. I have to be very careful to whom I reveal details about my former life. That's why this book is being written under a pseudonym.

Even among people who know me very well, I am occasionally reminded that they view me somewhat differently. I'll give you an example. Once, when I was visiting friends, after I had already been *frum* for a number of years, the phone rang. The person on the other end of the line wanted to know if a particular restaurant in the area had a reliable *hechsher*, kashrut supervision. "Just a moment," my friend's wife said, "Ben is here. He knows all about the local restaurant scene." I knew all about it from my frequent dates. She told me the name of the restaurant, and I told her it was okay. She passed along this information. There was a pause as she listened to the response. She then said, "Do I know of anyone else who would know? Let me think..." I was hurt.

Over the years I have felt hurt by a lot of little things. I remember once that a friend of mine kept telling me over and over how his daughter had gone out with a *baal teshuva*, as if to say, "You see? We don't hold anything against him just because he is a *baal teshuva*." Perhaps I'm being oversensitive. I don't know. On the other hand, I have heard this from so many friends who are BTs. Actually, you are the first BT I have met who has not had this experience.

Q: Maybe it is because I was weaned on the British class system. I wouldn't expect that someone from the aristocracy would marry into the working class, so I guess I'm not that concerned if the FFB class wouldn't marry a BT.

A: But don't you see you have just said the same thing? You have said that the BT is a lower class. Doesn't that bother you? Even an Englishman wants to be a member of the ruling class, not one of the natives.

Q: It's not a lower class really. It's a different class. Let me tell you why I am not as hurt by this as you are. Because a *frum*-from-birth Jew mixes with his own kind of people. They share the same culture. They have the same background. They know each other. They know each other's families. They feel comfortable with them. They know where they came from, and they know which direction they are heading in their Jewish observance. I can accept these lines of demarcation without getting upset about it. I know that I can never be the same as the Jew who is *frum* from birth. I know that I am different, and it doesn't bother me. I know that I look at Judaism differently.

A: Differently, I can accept. But do you think that you are inferior?

Q: Certainly not! I think that as a *baalas teshuva*, I am far more passionate about Judaism than many Jews who grew up in a traditionally Jewish home. I think there is a fire that burns in every BT that makes him more intense, and maybe this is what frightens the *frum* Jew. But I feel that this fire is the fuel that propels the BT from his former life to his new life.

Teshuva, repentance, can transform a person, but

will not usually erase past experiences from his memory. What's done is done, and what was said has been said. But it is these memories that give the BT the strength and the purpose to move forward — to carry on — often against all odds. And again, speaking for myself, the only way I could surmount all the pitfalls and obstacles was to become a fanatic — a religious zealot, if you will. I felt myself literally burning for Judaism. Like the fire that ignites a space shuttle and sends it hurtling up into space, I felt that I, too, was given the power to rise up and conquer the material forces that had tied me to the earthly things for almost all of my life. So I think there is a tremendous advantage in being a *baal teshuva*.

Incidentally, I must confess that I hate this term. It offends me deeply, and I try to avoid it whenever I can, because it makes me feel like a criminal.

A: Welcome to the club. I see that you are not really an exception to the rule. If the term offends you, it is because you also feel its negative connotations in the *frum* world. I have a feeling that your stiff British upper lip has also had its share of quivering in pain.

Q: There is one scenario that is a deep source of pain for me. Do you really want to know what it is?

A: Yes.

Q: Now don't laugh.

A: I wouldn't dream of doing such a thing.

Q: It's connected to photo albums. When my *frum-*from-birth friends take down their family albums, saying, "Would you like to see the pictures from our latest *simcha*?" then my BT antenna start quivering.

A: Why? I love photographs. I love to take pictures, and I also love to show them. Remember the Fourth of July on Governors Island?

Q: I love photographs too, especially of religious Jews before the Second World War. It doesn't bother me to see pictures of Jews from prewar Europe, like those taken by Roman Vishniac, for example. I feel connected to these Jews. Yet it does bother me to look at the albums of my FFB friends.

A: Why?

Q: I really don't know.

A: I wonder if it's because, in a way, you have something in common with these prewar European Jews: they only have a past. They have no future, and you seem to feel as if you have no past.

Q: Yes, I think you're right. Did you study psychology as well as engineering?

A: Only Psychology 101, but I can identify with you, because for a time I felt the same way. I also felt that I had no past or future. Some years back, I was able to learn more about my ancestors, and fill in the gap. It made a great difference to me; I felt as if I had roots. And now that I have children, I also feel that I am building a future.

Q: For me, it's different. I know almost nothing of my ancestors, apart from their names that are listed in my father's family Bible going back to the eighteenth century. I became *frum* as a mother of teenage daughters, so I can't exactly say I'm building a future. Even in the best relationships, teenage daughters are not all that interested in what their mother has to say, particularly if their mother has become a "religious fanatic." I daven that they will find their futures with us, but it's up to them and their children to find the right path.

And so, when I see the continuity of Jewish families, I feel a lump in my throat. My friend opens up her album, and there are shots of the baby's bris, the first haircut or his first day in cheder. Here are group photos of the *chasan* and *kalla*.

Naturally, her family consists of only respected rabbanim, and, of course, his family can trace its lineage back to the Vilna Gaon. There they are, staring at me from the pages — uncles, nieces, nephews, brothers, sisters, all wearing religious garb — bearded men, so solemn and aristocratic, the women dressed so modestly. I turn the pages, uttering the required, "What *nachas*! May you all live and be well! How beautiful! How handsome! How blessed!"

I come to the final page, close the book and start to tell my friend about my children and my grandchildren. After all, I am a mother and a grandmother too, and like all mothers and grandmothers, I am proud of my children's accomplishments. They are not observant, but they are fine, good and decent people. And yet, because they are not *frum*, no one ever seems to want to hear about them. No sooner have I opened my mouth to tell of the latest events in their lives when my friend's eyes glaze over, she starts to fidget, and mutters, "Excuse me. Something's bubbling over on the stove in the kitchen." She runs out of the room, leaving me in midsentence.

A: How terrible!

Q: Granted, it doesn't happen very often, but when it does, I am hurt by this insensitivity.

A: Have you ever said anything?

Q: No, I just sit there thinking how wonderful it must be to have roots, to be connected, to have a past. I feel a tremendous sense of loss and longing. I feel like a Jewish orphan.

A: Now that the truth is coming out, is there anything else about being a BT that bothers you?

Q: Yes, there is something else that is even more painful than the photograph albums. *Baruch Hashem*, in Judaism, there are so many *chagim*, holidays, throughout the year, and I know that we are commanded to be joyful. But it is hard for me to be joyful when everyone is with his family, and I cannot invite my family to be with me because I know that if I do, they will drive to my home. Going to their home is out of the question since they don't keep kosher, and they are not *shomer Shabbos*. Therefore, rather than being a joyful time, for me the holidays are always laden with regret and longing. I know my children don't like the situation, either. They know I am hurt, but this doesn't make it any easier for me. I keep thinking, "If only my children would become *baalei teshuva*, so many difficulties would be resolved."

A: How do you manage these difficulties in the meantime?

Q: I tread carefully in order not to hurt their feelings. I watch what I say. I don't want them to feel that I am trying to pressure them. I have to watch my Ps and Qs, otherwise I may end up pushing them away from Judaism. They do have a sense of Jewish identification, but only up to the point where it won't impinge on their desire to "do their own thing." Don't misunderstand. They are wonderful children, and are so good to me in every other way.

You have spoken about your complicated relationship with your own family, but I think it's harder for me. You were young when you set out on your journey; I was already a mother with teenage daughters. You have built up a family; I have, in a sense, lost mine. I also carry a burden of guilt.

Perhaps I am at fault. When the girls were growing up, we moved to a non-Jewish neighborhood. There was a tremendous drug problem in the public schools. To protect my children, I enrolled them in a private all-girls Catholic school with a sterling academic reputation. Only the best families sent their children to this school. How could I compete with the peer pressure to conform? I could hardly drag them by the hair of their heads to go to shul. And so, I left them to their own devices while I became more and more religious.

A: How did they feel about your becoming a *baalat teshuva*?

Q: As they got older, they approved. They still do. I would even say they are proud of me. They feel that my choice was right for me, but they refuse to entertain the idea that it is also right for them and for every Jew.

From time to time, I tell them about my concern for their spiritual well-being. They respond by saying, "Don't worry about us. We are fine as we are." I tell them, "I'm not talking about your physical well-being, I'm worried about your *neshama*, your soul."

To them, today is what counts; tomorrow will take care of itself.

A: I know BTs who became BTs when their children were already grown up, and I see that they are more accepting of their children than you are. They realize that not having been raised *frum*, their children really don't understand what it's all about. Their expectations are not as high as yours seem to be.

Q: I am less understanding. Probably years of anti-missionary work for Yad L'Achim have made me less tolerant. I also believe that the reason I am not so forgiving is that my children do know the right path. They have watched my progress over the years; they are not completely ignorant regarding Jewish practices. They do keep some traditions, so long as they are not too hard and are fun to do: the Pesach seder, Chanuka with latkes, Purim with *hamentaschen*.

My grandchildren in Canada have received a far better Jewish education than I; they studied at the local Jewish day school. They cannot claim, "We don't know any better!" Now my only grandson will be entering college, and then what?

A: Don't you think you should be encouraged by the fact that they did receive the rudiments of a Jewish education and that they have a *frum* grandmother?

Q: Yes, you're right, but... Just a moment! I think we've forgotten who is interviewing whom! Let me just sum up by saying that while it hasn't been a bed of roses, we Brits never expect a bed of roses — at least we didn't when I was growing up.

A: But I don't think we have to ask people to accept a bed of thorns either.

Take a Jew who is twenty and single. He has a group of friends, good friends. He has a good relationship with his family. One day, seemingly out of nowhere, he begins to feel the pull toward his roots. He tries a little *Yiddishkeit*, and he finds that he is being drawn in further and further. One day, he notices how far he has moved from the people he grew up with. There is a wall separating him from them. Their concerns are no longer his concerns. His interests have nothing in common with theirs. He realizes there is no going back. He wants this new world, but what does he find? He finds that many in this new world look at him with disdain. What should he do, call up his mother and cry? She'll tell him to forget all this nonsense. But he knows that despite everything, it isn't nonsense.

There's no one to talk to. Who are you supposed to talk to? Who do you cry your heart out to? Here you are. Most of your friends are gone. Your old world has been destroyed, but you have not yet built a new one. You are all alone, and you are just twenty years old! You feel increasingly disconnected from your old world. It is at this point that the *frum* community should be pulling you in, putting its arm around your shoulder and saying, "Yes, you have entered a new world with new friends. We accept you. We want you. Welcome home."

When I was living in Jerusalem, I went to the annual Purim play put on by the boys at Ohr Somayach. Their plays are very well done and always extremely popular. This particular play was a spoof on "The Wizard of Oz." The quest to gain admission to the wizard was replaced by a quest to be admitted to the Mir Yeshiva. Just as the wizard could make one complete, so, too, would admission to the Mir turn the boy from Ohr Somayach into a real *yeshiva bocher*. Most of the audience seemed to have a good time. I was sitting next to Rabbi Bulman, and he asked me what I thought. I told him, "I see here tremendous pain." With tears in his eyes, he said, "I agree."

Q: So what is the solution?

A: First of all, as you said, more sensitivity, and, I would add, more humility.

The tremendous responsibility of the teachers of the BT is another issue that we have not yet discussed. Almost all the rabbis I have met who are involved in this work are wonderful people who devote almost every waking moment to their cause. When I was living in Jerusalem, I became close to Rabbi Bulman and his wife, and spent a lot of time in their home. The phone was constantly ringing, people would drop in unannounced, each one with a problem requiring immediate attention. Rabbi Bulman gave of his time unstintingly, as if the person in front of him was the only person in the world and finding a solution to his problem was of cosmic significance.

A *baal teshuva* has to know who to ask. Preferably, the person should be someone of stature, who knows him. Otherwise, the advice he gets may not be the right advice for him.

Q: Can you give an example?

A: Yes, about a year or two after I started keeping Shabbos, I was faced with a difficult family situation. My aunt was taking care of my grandfather. Her daughter was about to marry a Catholic boy in a joint ceremony with a priest and a Reform "rabbi." I knew it would make for a very unpleasant situation if I did not attend the wedding, since I visited my grandfather quite often. I asked my friend Nathan what he thought I should do. He told me that in a tough situation like this, the thing to do would be to ask a rabbi with experience in these matters. Meanwhile, his wife had convinced me to sign up for a BT Shabbaton. A well-known rabbi was the scholar-in-residence. He was very involved in *kiruv* work. Nathan said, "Well, here is your chance. He knows all about the problems of *baalei teshuva*. Ask him what you should do."

The Shabbaton was nice. I enjoyed the rabbi's talks. On Shabbos afternoon, I asked him if I could speak with him for a while.

"No problem," he said.

We sat in the lobby of the hotel, and I began to tell him my story. I told him about my background and the problem at hand. After I finished speaking, he gave me his advice.

"Here's what I suggest," he began. "It would probably be best for you not to be so involved with your family. Otherwise, you might not remain *frum*. After Shabbos, write them a letter explaining why you can no longer maintain the relationship as it was in the past."

Q: What was your reaction? What did you do? Did you write the letter?

A: No. My reaction was, "That's not for me." I realized I had made a mistake by asking advice of someone who really didn't know me. After a brief conversation in a crowded lobby, how could I have expected him to know what was right for me? What turmoil I would have introduced into my life and the life of my family had I taken that advice!

Q: So you went to the wedding?

A: Fortunately, I decided to ask the rabbi of the small shul near where I lived what he thought I should do. He knew me, and he knew my background. He listened carefully. He didn't answer immediately. After mulling it over, he told me he didn't think it was permissible, but since it was such a delicate matter, he would like to refer it to someone more familiar with the nuances of the halacha. He would ask for a *psak*, a halachic ruling, from the *rosh kollel* of the out-of-town *kollel* where his son was learning. Perhaps he would be able to come up with an acceptable solution.

Q: What did the *rosh kollel* say?

A: He said I should not go to the ceremony, but that I should make an appearance at the reception. He recommended that I go in, leave for a while, and then go back in again. In other words, to be a part of it, yet not be a part of it.

Q: How did you explain this to your aunt?

A: The wedding was approaching, and one day, my aunt asked me, "Well, are you coming?"

I said, "I consulted a rabbi, and he said—"

"You asked a rabbi whether or not you should come to your cousin's wedding?" she interrupted in disbelief.

"Why not? If I'm sick, I ask the doctor what to do. If my car is broken, I consult a mechanic. If I have a question about life, I ask a rabbi what I should do."

"So — are you coming?" she asked impatiently.

"I won't be able to attend the ceremony," I replied, bracing myself for the reaction.

"Well, I hope at least you'll show up for the reception."

"Wouldn't miss it for the world," I answered.

I think humility and sensitivity are the two prime qualities needed in such situations.

When I was living in Jerusalem, a friend of mine who attended one of the yeshivas for *baalei teshuva* wanted me to meet a young woman he had gone out with. It hadn't worked out for him, but he thought she would be perfect for me. He pressed me to call the rabbi who had set it up. After finally reaching him, the rabbi asked me where I was learning. I told him that I learned in the evenings, but that I was working during the day.

"I know the girl and her family," he said, "and they are looking for someone who is learning full time."

I felt hurt. I felt I was rejected even before they found out who I was.

Another example. I was learning with my *chavrusa* one evening in New York when the Gemara described a shul in Alexandria that was so big they used flags to signal the people when to answer Amen. The next evening, I brought along with me a book from the Diaspora museum that showed a model of what the shul might have looked like. As we were looking at the illustration, the fellow sitting at the next table looked at me disparagingly.

"You may not realize it," he said, "but we don't bring books like that into the yeshiva."

Again, I feet that more sensitivity should have been displayed.

In our earlier conversations, we talked about feelings — the excitement of discovery, the emotional highs, the *hashgacha* — that is all part of the *baal teshuva's* journey. However, any discussion of what it's like to be a *baal teshuva* would be incomplete without addressing the pain, the hurt, the alienation, the feeling of always being on trial, that are also part of becoming a *baal teshuva*.

Q: Perhaps the *baal teshuva* should also be more open about his sensitivities.

A: I agree. People need to understand that sometimes a word, a look on one's face, or even a gesture can undermine the results of years of striving on the part of the Jew who is trying to return to his people.

Having said all this, I want to emphasize how very grateful I am to all the many people who have helped me along the way. While there may have been, here and there, some insensitivity on the part of our friends, the fact remains that we are forever indebted to them for their constant concern and support.

Q: I second that.

A: I was very fortunate because the Zs accepted me and treated me almost as if I was one of their children. This gave me a lot of strength to overcome the difficulties I faced. It also saved me from fitting into the mold of the stereotypical *baal teshuva*. However, not everyone is as fortunate. I feel that without an adoptive family, the Jew who becomes a *baal teshuva* in the *baal teshuva* yeshiva environment is almost guaranteed to be missing essential aspects of the *frum* personality. Judaism is meant to be experienced and absorbed in a home, not solely in a yeshiva. I wish that all *baalei teshuva* could have what I had.

Q: I know what you mean. I found this in the home of Rebbetzin Henny Walkin and her husband Rabbi Chaim Walkin in Jerusalem. They became my surrogate family. I practically lived in their house. Their daughter Ruthie willingly gave up her bedroom for me nearly every Shabbos, no small thing for a young girl to do. The seven Walkin sons treated me and continue to treat me with such respect. I am invited to all their *simchas*, and when I went to New York, I stayed with Rebbetzin Walkin's mother-in-law, who is a rebbetzin in her own right. Until I moved to Rehovot, I had a standing invitation to stay with the family in Bayit Vegan every Shabbos and every holiday. Now that they are grandparents many times over, their house is filled with their own grandchildren.

I can honestly say that I have experienced nothing but kindness, tremendous warmth and caring from this wonderful *frum*-from-birth family. Because of their caring, I was able to make a new life for myself in Rehovot, a small town, but one whose English-speaking *frum* community members literally open their hearts and their homes to every Jew, no matter where they stand, religiously speaking. Thanks to the Chief Rabbi, Rabbi Simcha HaCohen Kook, and his rebbetzin,

Nechama, I have been able to grow even more in my Judaism. I am indebted to them for welcoming me into their family and showing nothing but genuine concern for my well-being.

A: What you found with your "families" and what I found with my "family" is so vital to every *baal teshuva*!

Q: In my experience, though, I don't think every *baal teshuva* wants that. When I was in a *baal teshuva* seminary, I discovered that most of the women I met there were not interested in attaching themselves to a particular family. They liked drifting from one house to another, from one place to another place in Israel. They wanted to be free and independent.

A: Well, I think this is not healthy. A *baal teshuva* can wind up with a very unrealistic view of what a *frum* family should be unless he has been part of life in such a family. Otherwise, when they marry, they can have unrealistic expectations of what it means to raise a *frum* family. Maybe if they had attached themselves to one family, they would have a much more realistic view of things. They would see the relationships in an established *frum* family, and they would see that most children are not little Rashis at age four. A great deal of frustration and disappointment could be avoided.

A whole generation of young Jewish *baalei teshuva*, men and women, is being raised in an artificial environment. They don't get to see a parent reciting the Shema with his child; they don't get to see that there are children who sometimes refuse to say *birkat hamazon,* the blessings after a meal. When they get tired and irritable, they think there is something lacking in their spirituality, that something is wrong with them.

Q: Is it because they were not brought up with this?

A: Yes! It's because they never saw the real thing! But I did get to see the real thing. In a way, you might say, I was a *baal teshuva* who grew up in a *frum* family. I saw how they raised their children. I saw what it was like to be a Jewish father. Many *baalei teshuva* have unrealistic expectations because they did not have this experience.

Judaism is meant to be slowly absorbed in the warmth of a Jewish home. Is it any wonder that *baalei teshuva* often strike *frum* people as being different? Is it any wonder that *baalei teshuva* sometimes have strange misconceptions? Who is at fault? The *baal teshuva*? The *frum* community? Everybody? Nobody? I don't know, but I really think the solution is for every *baal teshuva* to be "adopted" by a family. He should have a place where he feels at home.

Q: Aren't you being a little bit unrealistic? My experience is that the *baal teshuva* requires a great deal of attention. They are like little children, and the majority of *frum* families have their own numerous children to tend to. Bringing a stranger into the house can be extremely wearing, and not every woman (because generally the load falls on the woman's shoulders) is equipped to deal with it. I know for a fact that I couldn't. Taking a *baal teshuva* into your home is similar to adopting a child. And don't forget that these are not even children. They are grownups who often carry a lot of emotional and psychological baggage with them. You could end up with some pretty strange characters camping out in your living room.

A: First of all, most *baalei teshuva* are not like children. They may need guidance and attention, but they are not children. Most are not kooks either. Obviously, being a BT's "family" may not be easy and is clearly not for everyone. However, I am sure that if you ask the Zs, or the Walkins or any of the other numerous families who have "adopted" a BT, you will find they will say they got at least as much out of the relationship as the adopted "child." I think the *baal teshuva* has something to offer. He is not a basket case.

Q: How do you propose to realize your dream? Would you advertise for adoptive families?

A: I think the way to start is to make people realize how important it is for a *baal teshuva* to have a "home." Numerous families who live close to BT yeshivot already invite *baalei teshuva* into their homes for Shabbos. This would be the logical place to start. Once these families realize the importance and the value of such a relationship, I am sure they would be on the lookout for a BT who would click with their family.

I also think the BT yeshivot need to impress upon the BT the importance of establishing a relationship with a single family rather than bouncing from place to place. I don't think this should be an exclusive relationship; I would not recommend that the *baal teshuva* become too dependent on his adopted family. However, it is very important that he have a "home" to introduce stability into his life.

Becoming a *baal teshuva* is difficult; it involves changes in every aspect of life. I don't think we can eliminate all difficulties and make the process of becoming a *baal teshuva* easy, but I do think we can make it easier. I am certain there are many *frum* people who are willing to help.

This fact is illustrated by a story I would like to tell you about my first meeting with Rabbi Bulman, which took place while I was still in the States.

Rabbi Bulman was on a visit from Eretz Yisrael and was staying in Monsey. A good friend of mine, Yoni, very much wanted me to meet Rabbi Bulman and arranged for us to spend Shabbos in the same house where Rabbi Bulman was staying. Yoni's father is also a rabbi, and the two families share a warm relationship that goes back decades.

While we were driving up to Monsey, Yoni said something very strange. "Don't be upset if Rabbi Bulman yells at you."

"Why on earth would he yell at me?"

"Well, if you say something he thinks is stupid, he will probably yell at you. He does that, but it is nothing personal. Don't take it to heart."

Leil Shabbos went fine. I guess I didn't say anything stupid. In fact, I think I made it a point not to say much of anything at all. I don't like being yelled at.

Shabbos afternoon, the house where we were staying was filled with people who heard Rabbi Bulman was in town. Rabbi Bulman was explaining the harsh realities that many *olim* had to face when confronted with the Israeli reality.

"The Israeli government pays a lot of lip service to aliya," he said, "but really it is just to satisfy their ideological needs. They need to talk aliya to justify the whole Zionist enterprise. They are for aliya, but when it comes to *olim*, that's another matter. They stick in their throat. They would prefer to have aliya without *olim*."

"Sort of like the *frum* community with b*aalei tshuva*," I whispered to Yoni, who was sitting beside me.

"Tell him. I'd like to hear what he has to say about that."

"With all these people here? He might yell at me!"

"Don't worry about it," he urged. "Go ahead — tell him!"

I hushed him, but he was undeterred.

"Rabbi Bulman, Ben wants to say something to you."

"No," I said, "I'd rather not say."

Rabbi Bulman said, "Please feel free to say what's on your mind. You're among friends."

"Well, you talk about the Israeli government's lip service to aliya, but it's the same thing with the *frum* community when it comes to *baalei tshuva*. It feels really good that there is a *teshuva* movement. It allows people to say, 'We were right all along. We were denigrated by the Maskilim, by the Conservatives, by the Reform, and look! Their children and grandchildren are coming babk to us!' They love the concept of a *teshuva* movement, but when it comes to the *baalei teshuva* themselves, the people, that's another matter. They would prefer to have a *teshuva* movement without *baalei teshuva*."

Rabbi Bulman didn't yell at me. He started to cry.

"Don't you think I am aware of the tremendous difficulties? You don't think I agonize over what we are doing to people, bringing them into a world where, in many respects, they are not wanted, where some will remain alienated for the rest of their lives? I ask myself, 'What am I doing?' But what can I do? Abandon them to a secular lifestyle? A Jew has to keep mitzvot, and I have to help him, no matter what the difficulties."

He assured me that despite the problems, many wonderful *frum* Jews do open their hearts and their homes, and, at the end of the day, most *baalei teshuva* will eventually feel integrated into the *frum* world.

"Everything you say is true," he told me, "and it hurts me, because I know how much it hurts you. But, you have to remember that there is another side to the story. Among the *frum* community, there are families that give a warm welcome to *baalei teshuva*, making them a part of their family. It may not be enough, it may not be 100 percent, but if you take advantage of what the *frum* community has to offer, you will make it."

11

" HEAD TALES "

Q: You mentioned that you started keeping Shabbos before you started wearing a yarmulke.

A: Yes, it was about a year after becoming *shomer Shabbos* that I started to wear a yarmulke.

Q: Since you had already come so far in your observance of Judaism, why did you wait so long?

A: As I said before, I did not want to make a public statement until I was sure that I could keep

Shabbos properly. I wore it at the Zs when I went for Shabbos, but I would take it off as soon as I left. I knew I should leave it on, but I just wasn't ready. I was very self-conscious about it.

The idea of suddenly appearing in public, especially at the office, with a head covering scared the living daylights out of me. I am a very private person. When I started my job, I was not *frum*; I didn't want to have to deal with my colleagues' reactions. I did not want to become the center of attention. So, I kept putting it off.

However, several things occurred over a period of a few months that finally caused me to make a decision.

I was on a business trip to Clearwater, Florida. On the plane, I was seated next to a real redneck couple, a husband and wife, real hillbillies.

We stowed away our baggage underneath the seats and in the overhead compartments, and settled ourselves in. I have a weakness for starting conversations with strangers in trains, buses and planes, which sometimes gets me into trouble. I opened up the conversation by asking them if they lived in Florida.

"Yes, we are from a small town just outah Clearwater, Florida, an' we jus' luv Florida," the wife told me.

"My aunt loves it too," I told them. "She just recently bought a place there to spend the winters."

"Near Clearwater?" he asked, "Y'all gonna visit her now?"

"No, this is a business trip for me," I answered. "She actually lives on the other coast, in Miami Beach."

"Oh," he said, "that used to be a luv'ly place, but it's been flooded now with people who just aren't our kind — if y'all know what I mean."

I had a feeling that I knew what he meant, so I just started to leaf through the in-flight magazine.

They were silent for a while, and then suddenly he asked me, "Y'all ever been a'huntin'?"

"Can't say I have," I replied.

"Neither has my grandson," he says. "That good fer nutin' father of his is gonna turn him into a real sissy!"

Trying to change the subject, I ventured, "Were you vacationing in New York?"

"Oh no, we are actually returning from a church trip to the Holy Land," the woman replied. "It was such a beautiful experience. Our pastor led the tour and explained everythin'. We went to all the holy sites — in Jerusalem, near the Sea of Galilee. It was such a joy to be in the land of the Bible."

The man was nodding his head vigorously as his wife spoke.

"It's a beautiful place," he chimed in. "Just a cryin' shame it's filled with all those kind o' people — if y'all know what I mean. You know, the same kind that ruined Miami." He continued talking about his trip to Israel, "They have all these signs in Jewish all over the place. They write it in the wrong direction, y' know, and all the letters look the same. They all look like squares. It's a wonder anyone can read them!"

Q: Didn't you say anything? I can't imagine keeping quiet in the face of such provocation.

A: I am always curious as to what these people think. Without my *kippa*, I felt as if I was travelling incognito.

The man went on, "And the people — they are so rude!"

"Rude?" I asked "How so?"

Moving closer to me and lowering his voice somewhat, he said, "Well, we entered through Jordan. Their airline is a lot cheaper than anyone else's. It's a lot cheaper than that Jewish airline where they grab the money hand over fist. Most of these pilgrim tours go to Jordan; it saves a lot of money, and it's pretty darn close to Israel. Only problem is, they make you stay overnight in Jordan, and there ain't a heck of a lot to do there. Guess they wanna get a bit o' yer money 'fore them Jews take it all. Heh, heh. Anyways, when we got to the border, there was this young Jewish gal, a border guard, and I told her, 'Now you see here, missy. Don't y'all stamp our passports with your Israeli stamp. We don't wanna get stuck in Israel. The Jordanians won't let us back into Jordan with an Israeli stamp in our passports, an' when we leave, we need to get otta here through Jordan.'

"And do you know what that Jewish border gal sez to me?" he continued.

"Do tell," I said to him.

"She sez, 'I won't stamp your passport, but don't ya' *ever* mention the name of that country to me!' Now what d'ya think o' that?" he said, snapping his thin lips together with a scowl on his face.

I wasn't sure I understood. "What name? What country?" I asked.

"Why Jordan!" he spat out, adding contemptuously, "Now who do they think they are, those Israelis?"

Just then the stewardess walked up the aisle, stopped at our row, leaned toward me and said, "We'll be serving you your kosher meal in just a moment. Sorry for the delay, but there was a slight problem with..."

Q: They must have died of shock.

A: No. Apparently, they didn't even know what kosher was. They looked at me curiously as I tried to tear the foil wrap off the scalding hot containers without any of the food landing in my lap.

"Y'all on a special diet?" the woman asked me.

"You might say that," I responded.

Their food trays came soon after, and we finished our meals in silence.

As the plane started to descend, I pulled from my carry-on luggage a newspaper in Hebrew with "all those letters that look like squares." You should have seen their jaws drop!

Q: What does all this have to do with your decision to start wearing a *kippa*?

A: Not very much, but isn't it a fitting coda to the end of my life as a bareheaded Jew?

Anyway, when I arrived at the hotel in Clearwater, Nathan was there. He was on the same business trip and had brought along his wife and youngest son, Dovid, who was about four or five years old at the time. I joined them in their room for supper. Dina had brought along a big salami from home and was slicing it and making sandwiches. I had forgotten to bring a *kippa*, and this did not go unnoticed by little Dovid.

"Where's your *kippa*, Ben?" he asked.

I went a little red, gulped and said, "Uh...well...um...I only wear it on Shabbat."

"Oh," he said. He just accepted it. But I felt bad. I realized that although it might be embarrassing to come to work with a *kippa*, it was even more embarrassing to not have one on in front of my little friend.

Q: And so that's when you started wearing a *kippa*?

A: Not yet. I was not quite there, but I was almost there. Soon after the trip to Florida, the pope invited Yasser Arafat to the Vatican. *What a chutzpa!* I thought. *He is not embarrassed to meet with this murderer?* And somehow I connected the two in my mind. "Why should I be embarrassed to wear a kippa?" I asked myself.

I decided that the next day, my kippa would become a part of my attire. I had to show the world that I was a Jew — a proud Jew.

Q: What was the world's reaction?

A: There I was, still living at home with my parents, and about to make this big statement. I used to wear my *kippa* at home to daven Shacharis and to eat breakfast. I would always remove it after *bentching*. My mother saw that this morning, I did not remove my *kippa*, and that I was about to leave for work.

"Do you know you forgot to take your yarmulke off?" she asked me.

"No," I said, "I didn't forget to take it off."

A worried look appeared on her face, and she said apprehensively, "You're not thinking of wearing it all the time now, are you?"

"No," I said, "I think I'll remove it when I take a shower."

"Listen," she said to me, "you are going to make yourself a lot of trouble by wearing a yarmulke in public. Not everybody likes Jews."

"Is that a reason not to wear it?" I challenged her, "If I had any doubts, you've just resolved them for me."

"Me and my big mouth," she said. Then she added in exasperation, "What's going to be next with you?"

My mother's fears were not unfounded. Someone spat on me on Governors Island when I started wearing the *kippa*. Another time I was walking with my *chavrusa*, Moshe, in Boro Park on the Fourth of July. He was telling me what a nice place Boro Park was, and I was telling him that my goal was to live in Jerusalem. Just at that moment, a car passed; there were a group of thugs inside throwing firecrackers at the *frum* passers-by. One exploded near our ears. After the ringing subsided somewhat, I turned to Moshe and said, "What were you saying about Boro Park?"

On another occasion, I was standing near the

yeshiva in my neighborhood when a bunch of hoodlums passed by with a sack of florescent light bulbs. One nonchalantly drew a light bulb from the bag and tossed it at me. Shards of glass flew around me, but, *baruch Hashem*, I was not hurt.

Q: What happened when you walked into the office for the first time with a *kippa* on your head. By the way, what color did you choose for this auspicious occasion?

A: I think the kippa was brown; I'm sure the face was red. Anyway, as I drove to work I was playing over the various scenarios in my mind. As I pulled into the parking lot, I thought to myself, *Well, here I am. How will my coworkers react?* I sat in the car for a few moments, feeling slightly sick from the anxiety. "Here goes!" I said to myself as I locked the car and walked toward the plant gate.

I imagined that I would enter the office, drums would roll, music would blare and a spotlight would be focused on my head. Everyone would look at me in astonishment, and their jaws would drop as I slowly sank through the floor.

In fact, it was not like that at all.

I walked into the office, and my supervisor, Mike, was the first to greet me.

Eyeing my *kippa*, he asked, "Is it a holiday today or something?"

"No," I said.

Then he asked, "Is this just for today, or is it a permanent addition?"

"It's a permanent addition," I replied.

"Oh. Okay," he said and returned to his work.

Then Bob, an older worker and a jolly fellow, came out of his office, "Hey, look at you!" he said in a loud voice. "What, you put a halo on? Are you trying to be more holy?"

"Well," I said hesitantly, "I guess we all ought to try."

The next one to appear was Lou, the department head. He came out of his office to see what all the commotion was about. He took one look at me, shrugged his shoulders, turned around, and then walked back into his office.

And that was it! No drums! No music! No spotlight! Just relief! And once again I learned a very important lesson, the same lesson I had learned when I told them I couldn't work on Shabbat. Sometimes, when you have to face something, you make it into such a nightmare in your mind that it paralyzes you and prevents you from doing what you know you must. The fears are always worse than the reality. You have to just jump into the water, like Nachshon, who jumped into Yam Suf before the waters parted. If you just do what you have to, you will discover that it is much easier than you thought.

I think this is a problem for every *baal teshuva*,

indeed, probably for everybody. Also, I have found that people, even non-Jews, are much more accepting if approached with respect and in a non-confrontational manner. And even if they are not, so what?

Q: Did your colleagues treat you with more respect once they saw that you were really becoming religious?

A: Not really. No, I don't think so.

Q: Did they ask you questions such as: Why? How? What?

A: I don't recall that they questioned me at all on this. Don't forget, it was a gradual process. They knew that I started to leave early on Fridays, they knew that I went to the Zs for Shabbat and holidays. Actually, I do recall one coworker telling me that he couldn't stand being with family on holidays and how terrible it must for me to have to suffer with two families. But, I think I had the respect of my colleagues before I became religious, and I think I had their respect afterward.

We had another business trip soon after I started wearing a *kippa*. We traveled to St. Paul, Minnesota, which has a large Scandinavian population. I went with my manager, Mike, an Italian with curly black hair. We were in a meeting filled with blond blue-eyed Vikings.

Mike, motioning toward the *kippa* sitting on my

head, whispered, "You must feel very out of place here!"

"Not at all," I answered. "Actually, I was thinking the same about you!"

"Me?" he asked in astonishment. "Why should I feel out of place?"

"Well," I replied, not missing a beat, "you're the only one here who doesn't have blond hair."

On another occasion, I had to go to some company meetings in Salt Lake City, known for its Mormon population. During a break in one of the meetings, a man, apparently with a position in the Mormon Church, came up to me.

"You see that fellow standing over there?" he asked, pointing to a tall man at the end of the hall, "He's one of our best missionaries. And don't think that that little beanie on your head is going to protect you!"

"Don't you worry," I answered. "This little beanie has been protecting us for thousands of years!"

12

" Finding My Way "

Q: It's 1987. You've been keeping Shabbos for a year. You just started to wear a *kippa*. You now identify as an observant Jew. What came next?

A: It was about this time that I realized I could not remain on Governors Island. I knew that my further progress depended on my becoming part of a Jewish community. I made several inquiries and thought about my options. One possibility was to move to the community where the Zs lived. Another was to move to Flushing, which also had a nice Jewish community and the added bonus that it was closer to work. In the end, I decided it was not a good idea to move close to the Zs. I wondered if I wasn't becoming too dependent on them.

Flushing had other attractions. I already had a good friend from work, David, who lived there. Dina's brother lived there. Most importantly, Nathan's oldest son, Ezra, was learning in a yeshiva there. So, I bought a co-op in Flushing.

Ezra used to invite his friends to his parents' home for Shabbos. Although I was quite a bit older than they were, I became friendly with some of the guys. One of Ezra's friends was Yoni. He and I hit it off right away. When he learned that I was planning to move to Flushing, he asked me if I would like to learn with him. Of course, I jumped at the opportunity and we started learning Gemara *Berachos* the first night I moved in. Although I am an orderly person who needs everything to be in its place, I tried to close my eyes as I passed the stacks of cartons, so that I could give top priority to learning. I knew that once I decided to do something that has to do with Torah studies, I had to start doing it no matter what. Had I delayed, I understood that my ardor would likely cool down. I told myself, "There are always things to be done, and if you don't start right, then you won't start at all." It took me more than a year to unpack my boxes.

Yoni and I made a great team; we learned very well together. We were both curious people. I always felt comfortable with him, although we came from very different worlds. While he had been attending cheder, I had been going to a church Sunday school. Nevertheless, he respected me. He accepted my unusual background, and didn't look down on me. It was not a one-way relationship, either; we learned from each other.

I would come home from work, Yoni would often join me for a quick supper in my apartment, and then we would be off to the yeshiva for the rest of the evening.

Q: Which kind of a yeshiva was this?

A: It was a yeshiva where most of the boys were from *frum* families, although there were a few who had been *baalei teshuva* for a number of years. The yeshiva was associated with a college. This enabled the boys to receive college credits, and attend classes part-time. Most of the boys there wanted a strong yeshiva education, but their parents wanted them to get a college degree. So this arrangement worked out for everyone.

I wasn't officially enrolled in the yeshiva, but I became a fixture there in the evenings and on Sundays. I loved the yeshiva atmosphere

I really enjoyed learning with Yoni. He knew so much. I could not believe how whenever the Gemara quoted a verse, he knew exactly where it was. "Oh yes," he would say, "that's in *Yeshayahu*, chapter twenty-two. This is in *Divrei Hayamim*, chapter eighteen."

"Wow, Yoni, that's really amazing!" I would say. I was extremely impressed. "How is it that whenever the Gemara quotes a verse, you know exactly where it is?"

"It's just a matter of experience. I'm sure that one day you will also know exactly where the verses are," he reassured me with a trace of a smile.

One evening in the yeshiva, I was waiting for Yoni, going over what we had learned the previous night, and I noticed for the first time that the references to the verses were printed in the margins! I chuckled to myself and decided that I would bide my time to seek revenge.

A few nights later, I came to the yeshiva a bit early and decided to take advantage of the fact that Yoni was a little late. I went over the section we would be learning that night. There was a rather complex sentence, with words in Aramaic that rarely appear in the Gemara. I did not understand it in the original, and so I searched for the sentence in a Hebrew translation.

Q: In Hebrew, you could understand it? You were that far advanced?

A: Yes, thanks to my years at the *ulpan*. It said that Bilaam was able to discern the moment of Hashem's anger because it coincided with the rooster's coxcomb changing color. I wasn't exactly sure of what this meant, but I knew the moment of my revenge had arrived.

Yoni arrived, sat down, and we started learning. I could barely contain my excitement when we reached this sentence.

"Don't fret about this one," he reassured me, "It's really hard! Even people who have been learning for years would have trouble with it."

"What's the problem? Seems simple to me," I said and proceeded to translate the sentence with remarkable ease.

"Wow!" Yoni exclaimed, "How did you ever manage to figure that one out?"

With a shrug of my shoulder, I said, "Elementary, my dear Yoni. I read the reference note in the margin, just like you've been doing."

We had a good laugh, and continued on with our learning.

One evening, around Pesach time, I mentioned to Yoni something about Pesach that I had read in Eliyahu Kitov's *The Book of Our Heritage*.

Yoni said, "That's not right. I think you must have misunderstood what he wrote."

"I don't think so," I replied, "but just a second, let me find it."

I went to the shelf, picked up the book and brought it back to the table.

Q: Oh! Was that the same book you had purchased from that wonderful Rabbi Shimoni?

A: Yes, and I think some of the pages had already started to fall out. Anyway, as I was leafing through the pages, Yoni said, "Do you know who translated this book?"

I ignored him because I couldn't find the passage I was looking for.

As I continued my search, Yoni repeated, "Do you know who translated this book?"

"Yoni," I said, "can you wait just a second? Give me a chance to find it."

"Okay, okay!" he said, but he just wouldn't give up.

"Ben," he asked again a few seconds later, "do you know who translated this book?"

"Look, Yoni, who really cares who translated it? Can't you just let me find what I'm looking for?"

I was getting very frustrated and annoyed.

"Just take a second to look. Please do it for me," he said, "and then go back to your search."

"Okay, if you insist."

With my eyes rolling upward, I opened up the front cover and read out loud: "...translated by Nathan Bulman."

"So?" I said. "Who is this Bulman?"

"Only my father's best friend and one of the leading English-speaking rabbis around today. When I was living in Jerusalem, I spent nearly every Shabbos in his home."

""Oh," I said, without missing a beat. "it 's really a great translation."

It was really tremendous *hashgacha* that I met Yoni. Since then, I have had very good *chavrusas*, but the bond with Yoni was very special. He was the perfect *chavrusa* for me. I guess that spending so much time around *baalei teshuva* when he was a *ben bayis* by Rabbi Bulman made him very sensitive to my feelings. I felt, and still feel very close to him.

Q: You were obviously spending every free moment in the yeshiva. Did this have an effect on your studies at Lincoln Square Synagogue?

A: Yes, I had far less time now that I was in the yeshiva every night. You will recall that I had been taking courses with Rabbi Weiser at Lincoln Square. At the time of my move he was teaching a new course on Rav Dessler's *mussar* work, *Michtav Me'Eliyahu*. I had been taking a course with him on Rav Dessler before, and I would have continued, but I just couldn't juggle everything and so I very reluctantly dropped it.

One day, I mentioned this to Yoni.

"You enjoy learning Rav Dessler?" he said with excitement. "I do too! Let's learn it together!"

I had a nonreligious friend at work, Ed. He told me that his wife wanted to learn more about Judaism.

"What about you? You should also learn a bit. Why don't you and your wife both take a class at Lincoln Square Synagogue? They have great courses and teachers there. I'm sure you would love it."

He told me, "It's such a pain to get into Manhattan. We would have to take a bus and a subway. But if you should hear about anything local, let me know."

That evening, I told Yoni that I had a marvelous idea. Yoni would give a *shiur* on *Michtav Me'Eliyahu* in my apartment. I would provide the nosh: potato chips, pretzels and so on. To make a nice mix, we would invite both religious and non-religious people.

Ed and his wife started coming, and Ed, who always emphasized that he was coming more for his wife's sake, would come even when she couldn't make it.

It went very well, and we kept up the *shiur* for about a year. Yoni was very successful. People kept coming week after week, month after month and were very disappointed when we cancelled the *shiur* after he got married and moved away.

Giving the *shiur* helped to convince him that he should go into *chinuch*, which is something he wasn't even considering at the time. Today he is a very popular, highly talented and gifted rav. I derive some satisfaction that the *shiur* in my apartment inaugurated his rabbinical career.

Q: You sound as if you were really on cloud nine after your move.

A: Yes; everything was so exciting. I was in a Jewish community. I was learning. I had a *chavrusa*. I was keeping Shabbos. I felt that I was starting to see the fruits of a long struggle. I was sure that the hardest part was behind me. I was flourishing, I had arrived, and from hereon in, everything was just going to be fine. I would say that this was my honeymoon period.

Speaking of honeymoons, even in the area of *shidduchim*, things were going better. I had met someone, and we seemed to be enjoying each other's company more and more. She knew about my background, and had told her parents about me. Unlike many other girls I went out with, it didn't seem to bother her. I think her parents were a bit uneasy about my background, but it didn't seem to be such an insurmountable problem. Things couldn't have been going better until...

Q: Until...?

A: Until everything started to fall apart. First, the economy started to falter, and Nathan lost his job.

Working next to him for five years or so had had such a tremendous influence on my life. It was very upsetting for both of us. It was wonderful working with Nathan. The day was peppered with *divrei Torah*. He was also my mentor, and I relied on him for advice on all sorts of matters. After he left, I would look at his empty desk and feel absolutely miserable. He had left a terrible void. Actually, he had really left piles of papers on his desk — a terrible mess. I shoved them in empty drawers to give myself more workspace. But no matter.

Of course, I was still a guest in his home almost every Shabbos, but there was a problem developing there also.

Nathan's oldest son Ezra and I had become good friends right from the start. The first Gemara I ever learned, I learned with him. Together with his father, we learned *Navi* on Shabbos mornings. He eased my way into Flushing because he was learning in the yeshiva there. I taught him to drive and used to help him with his homework. I viewed him almost as a younger brother. We had a lot in common. He was growing up and trying to find his place as an adult, and I was trying to find my place as a *frum* Jew. We were both going through a transitional period. We had many heart-to-heart discussions that brought us even closer to each other.

However, soon after Nathan left his job, I got the feeling that Ezra was having growing pains and needed much more attention from his father. Shabbos was really the only time they had to spend together, and I sensed an underlying tension — that I was in the way. The warmth between us had dissipated.

At first, I was at a loss to explain it, but after a while, I understood. Many years before, my parents had sort of adopted one of my older brother's friends, Jamie Stevens. Jamie was having problems at home, and his parents didn't know how to deal with him. At my brother's suggestion and with his parents' agreement, Jamie basically moved in with us; my parents made a room for him in the basement. At first, my brother was pleased to have his friend in the house. However, as time went on, he began to resent him very much. He saw him as a rival. I was afraid the same thing would happen to me and Ezra. Although the Zs had become like family to me, I felt that Ezra's needs came first. I quietly eased myself out of the picture, making my visits much less frequent.

Q: Where did you go? What did you do? Did you have a backup system?

A: No. It was hard for me. The Zs had been my life preserver. I felt abandoned. My support system was crumbling.

At the same time, other things in my life were unraveling. I was very confused about my feelings for the girl I was going with. She was very nice, but deep down, I had the feeling that she really wasn't for me, and I broke it off. Then, Yoni got engaged and announced that he and his fiancée would be moving to Eretz Yisrael a few weeks after the wedding.

A few days later I was called up to the *sefer Torah* at the yeshiva. I started the blessing, but I couldn't remember how to finish it. The guys were prompting me, but my mind went blank, I stood there, embarrassed and confused. I wanted to run away and hide. I left the building as quickly as I could.

Q: Did you feel like giving up?

A: It was certainly the lowest point in my becoming a *baal teshuva*. My entire world was falling apart. My Shabbos home was gone. My friendship with Ezra had been undermined. My hopes for a future with the girl I had been seeing were dashed, and my *chavrusa* and dear friend was off to Eretz Yisrael. I had never felt so alone.

There was no one to whom I could go for support. I could not confide in my parents. What could I tell them? How could I share with my parents the emotional turmoil I was going through? I didn't want to tell Nathan what had happened between Ezra and me, because I felt that by leaving them alone, the problem might solve itself. I did not want to burden Yoni with my problems just before his wedding. I didn't belong anywhere. I was absolutely all alone.

Q: Did you ever stop and wonder, "Hashem, why is this happening to me?"

A: I did. I certainly did. All my struggles were like that unfinished blessing. I felt that I had come so far...

Q: And against so many odds.

A: Yes, and now I was all alone. I also felt abandoned by Hashem. He had led me by the hand every step of the way. And I asked myself, "Where is His *hashgacha* now?"

But I didn't give up; I pulled myself together. I pressed onward. I started to stay in Flushing for Shabbos. My friend David, from work, lived in the neighborhood. He had often invited me for Shabbos, but I had rarely accepted. Eventually, he had stopped asking so much. Now I asked him, "Does your invitation still stand?"

"Of course," he said with delight, "although we had just about given up on you. My wife told me that we'd never get you away from the Ziv's for Shabbos."

There was also a pediatrician, Dovid, in the neighborhood whose house was always open to everyone who needed a place. We became good friends, and through him I met a lot of people. I got closer to the rabbi who advised me on my cousins' wedding and also to the *rosh yeshiva* where I learned at nights. Also, I became much closer to Mark. He was also a *baal teshuva*, a great *talmid chacham* and a lawyer. He gave a *shiur* in Gemara and has had a great influence on my life, and how I look at learning. He had a large family to support, but despite this he spent every spare moment learning. This showed me that if one is completely dedicated to learning, it is nevertheless possible to make great strides, regardless of the constraints on one's time.

I found a new *chavrusa*, Moshe, and we also became very close friends. Later on, I found other *chavrusos*, Zev and Mordechai. And so, I slowly built up a new network of friends, a new support system, and in this way pulled myself out of this crisis.

Q: Wasn't this also *hashgacha*?

A: Yes, it was. But the *hashgacha* that I now felt was very different from the sort I had felt before. In retrospect, I think perhaps a *baal teshuva* in the early stages gets a super dose of *hashgacha*. He needs it to get started. But then, a different quality of *hashgacha* takes over, requiring a more active role on the part of the *baal teshuva*. Now I had to struggle; this made me stronger. Without this crisis, what *mesiras nefesh* did it take for me to be a *baal teshuva*?

Moreover, the independence and maturity that I gained though this crisis would later enable me to cope with the problems of leaving America to make aliya to Eretz Yisrael.

I didn't know it at the time, but my new connections would help me immeasurably in Israel. Dovid, the pediatrician, made frequent visits and encouraged me through the low points. David, my friend from work, was to make aliya before me, and sort of prepared the way. When I couldn't sell my co-op, Mark offered to take care of it so that I wouldn't have to put off my aliya. Jonathan and Brenda, who I met through David, became my neighbors in Jerusalem, and we cried on each other's shoulders as we went through the absorption process. We even co-signed each other's mortgages. Now that was really *hashgacha*!

Q: Let's get back to the present. What was happening with the Zivs?

A: I still went to the Zs, but mostly when Ezra was not home for Shabbos. After about six months to a year, Ezra found his way out of his crisis, and I started to go more often, but not as often as before. Now I also went to other friends. It was a painful episode, but I grew through it. It was very unhealthy to be so totally dependent on the Zs, but now, after our discussion, I realize that this incident helped me to achieve a certain balance and the proper perspective on what happened. Hashem had used this trauma to help me find my own way.

13

THE *SIYUM*

Q: It's 1989. You've been learning in the local yeshiva at nights, and you are nearing a new milestone. You are about to finish your first *mesachta* in the Talmud.

A: Yes, it took me and Yoni about a year to get through the first third; during the next year, my new *chavrusa*, Moshe, and I managed to complete it. So we were going to make a *siyum* to celebrate the event. At first, we thought we would just have cake. Then I found out that Yoni would be visiting from Israel around that time, so we decided to make it a bit more fancy.

I happened to be speaking to my mother a few weeks before the scheduled event, and I said, half-jokingly, "Hey, I'm going to be making a *siyum* in a few weeks. Do you and Daddy want to come?"

She asked, "What's a *siyum*?"

I explained that people make a celebration when they finish learning a complete tractate, and this is called a *siyum*. I was very surprised when she said, "I'll speak to your father and let you know."

I didn't think they would come, but a few days later she called me and told me they would like to attend.

With my parents coming, I wanted to make a really nice *siyum*. I decided we would make it a full sit-down meal. Then I started thinking, "This is a really big milestone for me. So many people helped me reach this point. I really should invite all of them."

As I listed all the people who had helped me over the years, I realized the enormous amount of *hashgacha* that Hashem had granted me. There was Rabbi Shimoni from the bookstore in New Jersey; Nathan and his family; Rabbi Weiser, my teacher at Lincoln Square; the head of the yeshiva where I learned at nights; the rabbi of the small shul that I davened at in the mornings; my friends in the yeshiva and in the community. My list grew to more than thirty people! I enlisted Dina to help me with the planning, because it was turning into something more like a small bar mitzva or wedding.

Q: Were you still in close contact with all those people?

A: No, not all of them. I had not been in contact with Rabbi Shimoni for a few years. I telephoned his store to invite him and his wife to the *siyum*. A woman answered the phone, but her voice did not sound familiar.

"Miriam?" I asked.

"Uh...no...uh...Miriam is not here," was the reply.

"Is Rabbi Shimoni around?" I asked.

"No, but he will be here this evening," she told me.

I hung up the phone and thought that the store must be doing well if now they could afford to hire help.

That evening, I called Rabbi Shimoni to invite him and his wife to the *siyum*.

Rabbi Shimoni was delighted to hear I would be making a *siyum*.

"I will be happy to come," he said, "but I have some bad news for you. Miriam died suddenly about a year ago from an aneurysm."

I was stunned. I spoke to Moshe, and we decided to dedicate the *siyum* to her memory. At the *siyum*, I recalled her sensitivity, how she recognized that Hashem had sent a young man into her store for more than a Hebrew grammar book.

Q: It must have been a marvelous *siyum*. It must have been so moving, so unique.

A: It was. I bought most of the food from a local caterer. Dina also made some salads, cakes and watermelon boats. It was a unique *siyum* in that I also made a large chart to explain a very difficult Rashi in the Gemara.

There is a very long Rashi that explains the origins of the secular names of the days of the week, how they are related to the planets, and the position of the sun when it was hung in the sky on the day of creation.

When we got to this Rashi, Moshe said, "Let's just skip this one. We'll never understand it. It has all this stuff about astronomy in it. Nobody understands it."

"My dear Moshe," I protested, "you should know that you are speaking to a former member of the Amateur Astronomical Association of Long Island. We will understand this Rashi!" With the help on an astronomy text I had, the *Encyclopedia*

Britannica, and a lot of work, we finally understood that Rashi. I made a poster, and during the *siyum*, I explained the Rashi to everyone who came.

At the *siyum*, I quoted the saying, "*L'Makom yesh harbe sheluchim*," meaning that G-d has many emissaries that He uses to accomplish His will. "It seems," I said, "that over the past few years He has sent quite a few of His many emissaries to help me." I especially thanked Nathan, Dina, Yoni and Moshe.

I was very gratified when Moshe spoke, because he mentioned that with my background, I brought a unique approach to learning the Gemara. "Who else," he asked, "would go to a botanical garden in Israel specifically to find a plant mentioned in the Gemara? Who else brings plants and vegetables to the yeshiva to cut up in order to understand what the Gemara is talking about?"

He recalled an experiment we once did. The Gemara mentions that if you have dill from which you have not yet tithed, and you soak it in water, then you must tithe the water. It explains that all the taste of the dill goes out into the water leaving the dill as tasteless as a stick. When we learned this, I said to Moshe, "Let's check it out!" I went to a vegetable store, bought some dill, put it in water, and, sure enough, all the flavor and color went into the water!"

Q: Were your parents excited about your *siyum*?

A: Well, my mother surprised me again.

She called me up a few days before the *siyum* and asked, "Do you want me to come with my hair covered?" She must have read somewhere that religious Jewish women cover their hair.

I said to her, "Do what you want. I can't tell you what to do. I have a hard enough time knowing what I should do."

She asked, "Will Dina and the other women you invited be covering their hair?"

I answered her, "Yes, without question."

She responded matter-of-factly, "Well, if they're covering their hair, then I will cover mine too."

She came with a colorful kerchief wrapped around her head. She looked a little like a bubby straight from the old country.

My father came wearing a yarmulke. When he saw Dina, he whispered loudly to my mother, "Why isn't she covering her hair?"

My mother scolded him in a similar stage whisper, "Seymour, don't embarrass me! Can't you see that she's wearing a wig!"

My father nodded, but then started to stare at Yocheved, Nathan's baby granddaughter.

My mother noticed him staring at her and said,

"Seymour, don't be ridiculous. Babies don't have to cover their hair!"

Q: It sounds as if your mother loved it!

A: Whether she loved it or not, I don't know, but she said to me afterward, "I grew up among Jews, and I never met Jews like this. Your *siyum* was wonderful."

Q: The more I hear about your mother's reaction to everything you have done, the more I have the feeling that she is not, deep down, really as committed to Christianity as she appears to be. She still seems very closely connected to Judaism.

A: I think so. I think there is definitely something there.

Q: And I think that you, in particular, have been the catalyst. You have awakened something that was lying dormant inside of her. What did your father say?

A: My father is not a man of words, but I think he enjoyed himself very much. At first, he sat in the back, but Nathan saw to it that he was seated next to the *rosh yeshiva* and the other rabbis.

My grandfather also came, and commented on how happy everyone looked. I would take him with me to the yeshiva from time to time, and he really enjoyed it. He was not religious, but he came from a religious home. I think the atmosphere awakened memories of his childhood.

Q: What did your grandmother say?

A: My grandmother died a few years before I moved to Flushing.

In any case, it was a wonderful *siyum*. Nathan spoke, the *rosh yeshiva* spoke. Both my *chavrusas*, Yoni and Moshe, also shared their thoughts.

Rabbi Shimoni was very moved by the fact that the *siyum* was in memory of his wife. When it was over, people were reluctant to leave. There was a spontaneous *rikud*, a dance, afterward. There was such a warm feeling! I have made other *siyumim* since, but I have never had a *siyum* as lovely as this one.

14

"My Grandfather"

Q: You were very close to your grandfather, weren't you?

A: Yes, our relationship was very close and especially so in the last years of his life. After my grandmother died in 1984, I made an effort to visit him at least once a week. He became one of my closest friends. I saw him as the last link in our family to a world that had been entirely lost.

His Yiddish name was Zusha, but he was known as Joseph. He was born in America. His mother,

Rivka, was the daughter of a rabbi from Slutsk. His father, Pesach, came from Mariampol. They were part of the first great wave of Jewish immigration after the assassination of Czar Alexander II in 1881.

I found an article, "The Russian Jew in America" from the July 1898 issue of the *Atlantic Monthly*. It was written by one of the most influential Russian-Jewish intellectuals of the first half of the twentieth century. In the article, he stated that the clarion call of the Jews in Russia in the wake of the pogroms was, "To America! To America!"

My great-grandparents heard the call and made their way to America. I think they met and married there. My great-great-grandfather did not share their enthusiasm for America. Most Jews called their new homeland "the *goldene medina*." Many religious Jews, and he was among them, considered America to be the *treife medina*. He was convinced that the land of opportunity would not be conducive to Jewish observance. However, after his wife died, he apparently had no family left in the Pale, and he reluctantly joined his children in America.

He arrived at the old Barge Office, at that time the entry point for immigrants, which was near the US Customs House at the southeast foot of Manhattan. His son-in-law met him. I think this was the first time they met. My great-great-grandfather took one look at him, and, before even exchanging any greetings, pointedly remarked, "I see beards also have trouble growing in America."

My grandfather told me that his father worked in the garment industry as a finisher. It was a stressful life, because each worker got paid according to the number of garments produced, and my great-grandfather's work, putting the finishing touch on the garments, was the most time-consuming step. His fellow workers would constantly be pleading with him to go faster, because they weren't paid until he had finished his work. They even accused him of taking food out of their children's mouths.

Another source of stress was how the employers related to their Sabbath-observant workers. Back then, a seven-day workweek was standard. The rule in the *goldena medina* was that if you don't come in on Saturday, don't bother showing your face on Sunday. Unlike most immigrants at the time, my grandfather's parents clung to Jewish observance. So, every week, my great-grandfather was fired. Sunday mornings, he would sit on a bench in Seward Park on the Lower East Side of Manhattan waiting for a garment sweatshop foreman looking for a finisher.

He refused to give up on Shabbos, but his heart gave out on him. He was bedridden for many years. He had three boys, and the support of his family fell to his wife, Rivka. She rented a pushcart and sold trinkets and dry goods.

When my grandfather's two older brothers were old enough to work, they took over the support of the family, "Enough of this!" they told my great-grandmother. "It's not respectable for you to work like this."

Once they starting working, only my great-grandmother continued to keep Shabbos.

My grandfather, who was very bright, won a scholarship to the School of Civil Engineering at Cornell University. At that time, it was very unusual for a Jew to go to college. There was only one other Jew at Cornell. He had been sent from Palestine to learn agriculture. The university is located in upstate New York, and, at the time, there was no Orthodox Jewish community nearby. This probably weakened my grandfather's Jewish commitment even more. His brothers would send him money for basic living expenses. He rarely came home, because it was just too expensive.

His brothers did very well, and by the time my grandfather graduated from Cornell in 1917, the family had moved up to the Bronx.

Q: Wasn't he drafted as a doughboy?

A: No, World War I ended before they could send him overseas. My grandmother used to joke that when the Germans heard that my grandfather was coming, they surrendered unconditionally.

One day, my grandfather's cousin, Celia, from the Lower East Side, came to visit, dragging along Pauline, her closest friend. My grandfather was just leaving, but, after taking one look at Pauline, he turned around on his heels and joined them at the kitchen table.

Pauline was not too keen on wasting an entire day visiting her friend's relatives, and so they had arranged that Pauline would kick Celia under the table when she had had enough. But it was Celia who was getting bored. My grandfather and Pauline continued to talk and talk, ignoring Celia, and eventually it was she who was kicking Pauline from underneath the table. Pauline kicked back but didn't budge.

Before they finally took their leave, my grandfather asked Pauline if he could call on her, and they set a date to meet. But, Pauline was somewhat forgetful. When my grandfather arrived for the date, he was surprised to see Pauline on the way out, accompanied by a fine-looking young man! My grandfather stood there, watching them leave, not knowing quite what to do. Pauline's father grabbed my grandfather by the arm and pulled him into the apartment.

Pauline's father, thinking quickly, said, "I'm so sorry, but my nephew unexpectedly arrived from out of town, and my brother would never forgive me if Pauline didn't show him the sights. Please sit down and have something to eat. You've come a long way."

My great-grandfather, Pauline's father, had decided that Pauline was going to marry Joseph, and he was not going to let his nineteen-year-old daughter's shenanigans get in his way. He escorted my grandfather to the door saying, "Again, I really apologize. Pauline will be in touch with you."

When Pauline came home, her father was furious. "What's the matter with you?" he asked. "We are not going to let this engineer get away. You are going to marry this young man!" He sat her down, and dictated to her what she should write on a postcard. She wrote that she was sorry for what had happened and that she would like to set another date. My great-grandfather didn't even wait till the morning to mail the postcard. He ran out in the middle of the night.

Before long, they were married, and the marriage lasted one week shy of sixty years when my grandmother died of heart failure in 1984.

Q: Did you ever discuss with your grandfather his feelings about your mother's conversion to Christianity?

A: No. My grandfather never directly brought up the subject, and neither did I. The closest he ever came to it was that once he remarked to me that he couldn't understand how anyone could believe in Christianity. He told me that the idea of a trinity was pure paganism, and the idea of a virgin birth was sheer nonsense!

Q: What was his attitude toward Judaism?

A: As I became religious, it awakened in him long-forgotten memories. When I would take him out for pizza in my neighborhood, he enjoyed putting on a *kippa* and showing me that he remembered the blessings. Occasionally, I would take him to the yeshiva, and he loved being there. One Purim, I took him there for the megilla reading. He also came to the Zs that year for the Purim *seuda*. He relished reliving his childhood experiences very much. When I took him to one of the *shteibles* in Flushing to daven, everyone there treated him like a king.

In the last two years of his life, his cognitive abilities were progressively impaired. One of the effects of this was that many of the defense mechanisms he had built up were stripped away.

Q: Such as?

A: Take his attitude toward anti-Semitism. He had always denied it existed. If I were ever to ask if he had had any problems being a Jew, he would dismiss the question with a wave of his hand. However, now, as he became less connected to the present, he started to recall his past. He told me the story of how his father lost his job every week. He told me how, when he was a boy, the Irish kids used to run after him and his friends, pelting them with bottles and stones.

I asked him, "What did you do?"

He said, "I learned to run. I learned to run fast. All my life I've had to run."

He told me how horrible his time was in college. He was one in a group of outcasts. This group included the Jew from Palestine that I mentioned, along with a few students from India and China. The other students used to torment them.

"Because I was so small," he said, "they enjoyed picking me up and throwing me into the lake."

Q: In an ivy-league college in America? I would not have been surprised if this had happened in England in 1917, but I was not aware that the same thing was happening in the land of the free and home of the brave.

A: People are unaware that before the Second World War, anti-Semitism was very strong in America, even, or maybe especially, among the intellectual elite. My grandfather told me that it had been a terrible mistake to go there, and how much he regretted it. What surprised me was that in all the years I knew him, he never even hinted at it. It was such a trauma, yet he had suppressed it all these years.

It was impossible for him to find employment as an engineer after he was awarded his degree. A Jewish engineer in those days was unheard of. Finally, he got a job in an engineering firm, but not as an engineer. His job was to keep the office warm by feeding coal to the stove. He would stay late, and after everyone went home, he would do engineering work at his own initiative and leave it on the boss's desk.

The boss started to give him work, but the other engineers in the firm were livid. They did not want to work with a Jew. So, they used to feed him the wrong information, and would try to trip him up in any number of ways.

"I went over my work dozens of times to make sure I had avoided their traps," he told me. In the end, he decided to take a government job, which would be more secure. Entry to these jobs was through civil service examinations, and it didn't matter if you were a Jew or not. Merit was the key, not religious affiliation. He eventually became one of the chief engineers in New York City.

Knowing how successful he had been, it was very hard to watch his mental abilities deteriorate. But now that he was unable to mask his true feelings, I was able to discover my real grandfather.

He also told me other things. My grandfather told me how his father had hired a rebbe to teach him. He told me of his mother's loyalty to Judaism, and how she remained observant her entire life. When I mentioned this forgotten fact to my mother, she recalled that when they visited her father's mother on Shabbos, they would always walk, and upon arriving would find candles burning and *challa* on the table.

When my grandfather reached the end of his life

and most of his memory had faded, these memories remained. Only they were important to him. In one of his all-too-rare lucid moments during the last six months of his life, he told me how happy he was that I had decided to live a Jewish life.

After my grandmother died, it was hard for him. He missed his wife of sixty years, but he managed to find things to keep him busy. He read a lot and continued the daily walks he used to take with my grandmother. He lived with my aunt, and although he was very appreciative of her care, he longed for his independence.

One day when I came to visit, he seemed very pleased with himself.

I asked him, "Anything special happen today, Grandpa?"

He responded with a chuckle, "I'll tell you, but you mustn't tell your aunt."

I said, "I'm making no promises, Grandpa. If you want to tell me, tell me; if not, not."

He took a deep breath and said with pride, "I took the subway to Manhattan today!"

"*You did what?*" I asked in astonishment. "You can't see well anymore. How did you know where to get off?"

"I just asked the person sitting next to me."

I admonished him, "You could have been hurt or killed! Don't you know that there are dangerous hoodlums on the subway?"

"No," he said. "I remember that a few years ago I used to see hoodlums on the subway, but today you don't see them anymore."

I said, "You don't see them, because you don't see well, but that doesn't mean that they're not there, Grandpa!"

"You have a point there," he admitted, "but don't tell your aunt. Why upset her?"

"No, we wouldn't want to do that, would we, Grandpa," I reassured him, "but please don't do that again."

But by 1989, there were subtle changes. My aunt told us that things were changing for the worse, but we were not living with him, and it was hard for us to see it.

My grandfather was about ninety-five at the time, and his children were also no youngsters. The family decided that the best solution would be to place him in an independent living center on Long Island, not far from where my uncle lived. It seemed to be a nice place. They had movies, a barber, a library, all sorts of activities. He seemed to manage well enough there for a few months, but his cataracts had gotten so bad that he was virtually blind. After he had surgery to remove the cataracts, his mental state rapidly deteriorated and a nursing home had to be found quickly.

He was placed in a nursing home in Queens, not far from me. I was happy about that, because it made it much easier for me to visit him. On the other hand, I was unhappy about the quality of his care. It was an impersonal, depressing place. I hated going there. I tried to take him out as much as possible. My grandfather either took it all in stride, or perhaps he just wasn't completely aware of what was going on. Often, he didn't seem to know who I was. He thought I was a friend. Once, when I took him to my apartment, we telephoned my mother.

"Oh, he said, "I'm here with…you know who," he told her.

He was frequently sent from the nursing home to the hospital. I was convinced that many of these hospitalizations were unnecessary, and that either the nursing home didn't want people dying there, or they got their fee this way without having to care for him.

In the summer of 1991, he became ill with pneumonia. He was usually sent to a hospital that was quite far from me, but this time he was sent to Parkway Hospital, not far from my apartment in Flushing. Now, I realized that I had the opportunity to fulfill a dream — to spend a Shabbos with my grandfather. There should be nothing more natural than a grandson spending Shabbos with his grandfather, but for me, it had never happened.

On Shabbos afternoon, I made my way to the hospital. We didn't have a table with a white tablecloth; there was no *challa* and no kiddush wine. Nonetheless, it was a Shabbos I will never forget

I visited him again a few days later, and he told me he thought he would live only another day.

"Nonsense," I told him. "Your fever is down. You're getting better."

"It's enough already," he said. "Do you know how old I am? People don't expect to live so long."

"Look," I told him, "I want you around. We'll go on walks. We have things to talk about. I want you to come to my wedding."

At this, he perked up and said with a grin, "Oh, you have news?"

"No," I said, "not yet."

"Well," he responded, "how long do you expect me to live anyway?"

"Thanks a lot, Grandpa," I muttered.

"No," he said, "you're right. Tomorrow will be better. Each new day brings new opportunities, new possibilities."

In December, he was again hospitalized. I visited him as much as I could. The last time I saw him was on a Thursday evening, and he was asleep most of the time I was there. At one point, he woke up, and caressed my face. I sat with him a while, but he didn't speak at all. When I told him that I had to leave and that I was going to daven Maariv at the yeshiva, he whispered, "I want to go, too."

That Shabbos, I was at the Zs. As soon as Shabbos was over, the phone rang. It was my mother. She gave me the bitter news: my grandfather was gone.

My mother told me that my uncle had called the local Jewish funeral parlor, on Shabbos, and told them that we wanted an Orthodox funeral. "Otherwise," he told my mother, "Ben will never speak to us again."

Q: And they answered the phone? A Jewish funeral parlor? I can't believe it!

A: Well, this is America. They handled funerals for all sorts of Jews. When someone specified an Orthodox funeral, they would call in the volunteers from the local *chevra kadisha*.

Dina called the rabbi who was responsible for the *chevra kadisha*, to make sure that they had been contacted.

I couldn't believe that Grandpa was really gone. He had always been there. Deep down, I guess I thought he always would be there.

I made my way to the funeral home to identify the body. It was hard. Very hard. When I arrived, they were not ready for me. I sat down in their waiting room and started to write a eulogy. As I wrote, I felt that it would be fitting for me, a grandson, to convey to my family and friends my feelings for my grandfather. I'd like to read it to you:

Eulogy for Zushya ben Pesach, z"l

25 Kislev 5657 / 28 Tevet 5752

My grandfather's Hebrew name was Zushya. Zushya is Yiddish for sweetness. Not only did Grandpa have a tremendous sweet tooth, but he also spread his sweetness to all who knew him. Even in his last months in the hospital, his sweetness and kindness drew people to him. Even when somewhat in a fog, he usually thanked and showed appreciation to whoever attended him. His gentleness attracted people to him, and his kindness shone even in the worst of circumstances.

A little more than seven years ago, his wife of sixty years, my grandma, passed away. Many of us here remember those long tension-filled hours as we sat with Grandpa in the waiting room. His reaction upon hearing of Grandma's death made a tremendous impression on me. He got up, walked over to the doctor, shook his hand, and thanked him, saying that he knew he had done everything possible. That was my grandfather.

The truth is that it was hard to get to know Grandpa. He was always so quite and unassuming. Grandma would hold court in her small kitchen, dishing up milk, cookies and stories. Grandpa sat on the step stool by the black wall phone, nodding his head whenever Grandma prompted, "You remember, Joe?" Sometimes he would tell a story himself; often not. You really had to work hard to see who he was, but the rewards were worth the effort.

He was also known by the name Joseph. Joseph means to add. He lived up to this name as well. He always added, and never took away. I never heard him speak harshly to his wife. His esteem for her seemed boundless. He deeply loved his four children, and I can't think of a time when I ever heard him criticize any one of them....

He always strived for peace. I don't think it was because he overlooked the faults in other people. I think that he never knew they were there. He loved his children's spouses as much as he loved his own offspring, to the point where I'm not sure he knew the difference. His grandchildren were dear to him, and G-d gave him enough years to even see great-grandchildren.

Like his namesake Yosef in the Bible, as an engineer with the docks and the building departments, he was deeply involved with public works. His talents were so respected that he was called out of retirement several times. In his late eighties, he told me that he thought that perhaps he would go back to work.

On a more personal level, let me tell you that over the last decade Grandpa was more than just a grandfather to me. He was one of my closest friends.

✶ My Grandfather ✶

He, the grandson of a Lithuanian Rabbi, was for me the last echo of an all-but-lost world. His childhood memories had elements of the world I was striving to recreate in my own life.

He took pleasure in my journey and shared my excitement as new worlds opened up for me and old memories revisited him. When he came over to my apartment for dinner, he would pop on a yarmulke and delight in showing me the blessings he remembered. When his vision was better. we used to read from the Torah or the siddur, prayerbook, together. Sometimes I would take him to shul, and we would pray side by side. One year, he joined in the Purim feast at the Zivs. He came with me to the yeshiva to hear the Scroll of Esther read by my friend Moshe. He loved it, but did remark that the megilla seemed longer than it when he had heard it as a boy.

When I completed my first volume of the Talmud, he came to the *siyum*, our celebration to mark the event, and he shared in the happiness of this accomplishment. A friend took him up to the *beit medrash*, where the young men in the yeshiva study, and he remarked on how happy everyone looked.

In recent months, I saw a side of him that perhaps many of you did not see. Last summer, while visiting him at the hospital, I told him, "I have to go now Grandpa. It's time to daven Mincha." He remarked, "You certainly have become quite religious, haven't you?" "I try," I told him. He looked at me, and told me that he was very pleased that I had decided to live the "Jewish way." This was the best way, he assured me.

The only time he was ever angry with me was when I came to visit him one Wednesday evening about a month ago. "Why are you here?" He screamed at me. "You're ruining it! Why did you come?" I wasn't sure he knew who I was. But he did. He thought it was Friday night.

Last Thursday night, the last time I saw him, he was extremely affectionate — caressing my face, touching me. He wanted to say something, but the words didn't come. As I put on my coat, he asked me where I was going. I told him I was going over to the yeshiva. "I want to go too," he said.

"Maybe you'll come with me soon, Grandpa," I said. "Purim is just around the corner. We'll listen to the megilla together."

It was not to be. But we Jews have a funny way of looking at time. The generations are connected backward and forward... Whether we are children, parents or grandparents; our souls are intertwined. By raising ourselves, we raise all the generations, past and future....

Before each parting, I would say to Grandpa, "*Chazak!*" He would respond by looking at me, clenching his fist, and translating in a firm voice, "Be strong!" May G-d give us the courage and the strength to extend ourselves, to be more than what we are, and to enable us to preserve the values that Grandpa held dear.

The next day, the family gathered at the funeral home. Nathan and Dina came with their children.

This didn't surprise me, but I was surprised to see that Dina's brothers and sisters also attended, especially as Dina's brothers are *kohanim* and had to remain outside. I was moved to see that my friends from the yeshiva came to pay their respects. I delivered the eulogy, and Nathan spoke as well. We arrived at the cemetery.

My friends from the yeshiva carried the casket to the grave, and together we buried him. I winced with each slam of the dirt on the casket, but I knew that we had performed one of the greatest mitzvot possible. My mother, her siblings, and the other grandchildren had remained on the sidelines, as if they were observers, and I worried, *Was I overstepping my bounds? Had we unintentionally taken over?*

Q: I am sure your mother and everyone there were greatly moved, and appreciated what you and your friends had done for your grandfather.

A: That's exactly how it was. My family was impressed by the beauty and meaning of the ceremony. A few days later, my mother called me and said, "I want you to know, I was talking it over with your aunts and uncles, and we remembered how horrible we felt at your grandmother's funeral. A rabbi who didn't even know her gave the eulogy, and then we walked away, leaving her body at the side of the grave for the cemetery workers to bury.

"We very much appreciated your words about

Grandpa," she said. "We also want to thank you and your friends for burying him with dignity. What a difference from when your grandmother died. Here, we walked at peace with ourselves, knowing that everything possible had been done for your grandfather."

15

"The Search for Harav Yaakov Moshe"

Q: Ben, your family is about as assimilated as any family can possibly be. And yet, there are so many things that happened to you in your journey — chance meetings with the right people along the way, for example, a wrong turn (that turned out to be the right turn) that led you to Rabbi Shimoni. I just can't help feeling that someone up there was rooting for you. Maybe it was your grandfather's grandfather — the rabbi from Slutsk that you mentioned.

A: I am too rational to think that my great-great-grandfather was guiding me. But I am not so rational that I will not admit to having the feeling that something was pulling me in, sometimes against my will. I can tell you that over the years I have developed a connection to my great-great-grandfather from Slutsk.

Q: What do you mean by that because…um…I mean, he's not alive anymore, if you don't mind me saying so.

A: When I started to search for his grave, he became a real person to me rather than just a name. Before my grandfather passed away, he told me that his grandfather was buried not far from his parents' graves, and that this grave had a relatively large monument. On other occasions, he described a grave of a "big rabbi" with a relatively large monument not far from his parent's graves.

I remember that in his living room, there was an enormous portrait of his grandfather, dressed in black, wearing a large rabbinical-looking skullcap, his right hand holding a *sefer*.

I remember as a child looking at this picture, and being impressed by the calm contemplative eyes. My older brother, on the other hand, used to be afraid of this picture. He claimed that great-great-grandfather's eyes were following him as he moved about the room.

I never asked my grandfather if the "big rabbi" he mentioned was actually his grandfather, but I had a hunch that this might be the case. I wanted to go with him to find the graves, but he passed away before we had the chance.

With his death, I felt that my one tenuous link to my Jewish past had been torn away from me. My grandfather was the only person closely related to me who had an understanding of who I am and what was motivating my return to Judaism. As I started to become a *baal teshuva*, I had to discover everything on my own. Judaism should be handed down from generation to generation. The past points toward the future. I had no past. I was a Jew without a past — a contradiction in terms.

A few months after my grandfather died, I became seized with the idea of reclaiming this past. I called my Uncle Eli, who used to take my grandparents to the cemeteries, and asked him if he remembered where my grandfather's parents were buried. He told me they were buried in Washington Cemetery in Brooklyn. I telephoned the cemetery office and asked the woman who answered the phone how difficult it would be to locate the graves of relatives who died between forty-five and one-hundred-and-ten years ago. She told me that if I did not know the dates of their deaths, their complete names, and their ages at death, it was almost impossible, since all the records were in handwritten ledgers.

I only knew that my grandfather's grandfather's first name was Yaakov. I once heard that his daughter's maiden name was Goldin, but I wasn't sure if he was known by that name. At this time, Jews used to change their last names almost as frequently as they would change their shirts. Usually, this was to escape the Russian authorities, but sometimes it was for other practical reasons. For example, when my grandfather's father, Pesach (Phillip) Goldstein (Harav Yaakov's son-in-law) immigrated, the immigration officer asked him to spell his family name. His family name was Rabinowitz, but he didn't know how to write in Latin letters. Thinking quickly, and pointing to the person who had just been processed, he told the immigration officer that they had the same name. And that is how Pesach Rabinowitz became Phillip Goldstein.

I knew the most about my great-grandmother, Rebecca Goldstein. My grandmother once remarked, "It was a shame that your grandfather's mother died before the Japanese were defeated, but at least she lived to see the defeat of Nazi Germany."

That chance remark enabled me to know that she died in the middle of 1945. I gave the woman on the phone this last bit of information, and she said she'd give it a try. She put me on hold, and a few minuets later told me that she had found a Rebecca Goldstein who had died on August 11, 1945. I told the woman that while it was possible that this was my great-grandmother, I could not be sure, as Rebecca and Goldstein are both common names. She asked me if she died in Morisania Hospital in the Bronx. I told her I didn't know, but since she did live in the Bronx, it was possible. She told me that although she wasn't allowed to give out details about next of kin, she couldn't see what harm it could do almost five decades later.

"Funeral arrangements were handled," she said, "by Morris Goldstein of 1890 Andrews Avenue in the Bronx." Immediately, a wave of emotion swept through me. Morris was my grandfather's oldest brother. In an instant, I felt connected to my great-grandmother whom I had never met; she was no longer an abstraction. I was told that the grave could be found at Cemetery 1, Post 58, Row 4, Grave 17.

That night, I called my mother. I asked her what 1890 Andrews Avenue meant to her. "It sounds familiar," she hesitated. There was silence for a moment, and then she said with surprise, "That's my late Uncle Morris' address! How on earth did you know that?"

I told her I was searching for her ancestors, and that I hoped to find their graves as soon as possible.

On July 2, I drove into Brooklyn with great anticipation. I was confident that I would find my great-grandparents' graves, and hoped that my great-great-grandfather's grave was really nearby, as my grandfather had remembered. I was very excited. I had built up this scenario in my mind that I would find his grave and that the monument inscription would testify that he was a great rabbi and the author of some important work. I would then search for his book in the great libraries of the world, I would find it and I would then be able to read what he had written.

Without too much difficulty I found Post 58. It was a fenced-in section. I walked through the gate, and found Row 4, Grave 17. I looked at the inscription on the stone: "Rebecca Goldstein. Died August 11, 1945. Aged 80 years."

The Hebrew inscription added more detail: "Rivka bas Harav Yaakov Moshe. Died 2nd of Elul, 5705."

I was so excited. I wanted to stay a while at the grave, but I decided I would come back later. I had to find her father's grave. I was sure I would find him. Now I knew my great-great-grandfather's name more completely. I was hot on his trail. I had known that his name was Yaakov, but, until now, I hadn't known that his middle name was Moshe.

Two rows away and a few graves down, I found Rivka's husband, my great-grandfather. I read the inscription: "*Ish tam veyashar*, Pesach ben Yaakov Tuvia. Phillip Goldstein. Aged 54 years. Died 15th of Cheshvan, 5680 (November 8, 1919)."

I gazed at the tombstone. I thought of how he had valiantly tried to preserve the values that he brought with him from Europe, the sacrifices he made for Shabbos. But his children had become

Americanized, abandoning almost all tradition and observance. He must have thought he had failed and that everything he held dear had been lost. However, here I was, his great-grandson, more than seventy years later, standing beside his grave. "All is not lost," I whispered. "I've come home."

It was hard for me to leave his grave, but I still had one more grave to find. Where was my great-great-grandfather? I systematically searched through the graves in the section, but was unable to find him. There were a few tombstones that were impossible to read due to the ravages of time. I assumed that one of those graves must have belonged to him. I left that section, disappointed, thinking that probably one of those graves belonged to him, and now I would never find the details I had hoped his tombstone would reveal: his father's name, when he died, how long he lived, and if he had written any *sefarim*.

Q: I suppose at this point you decided to give up the search and go home?

A: I was about to. However, when I passed through the gate to leave the section, I happened to notice an inscription above the gate that I had not noticed before: "Matte Levy, 1896."

This section contained graves for members of the Matte Levy society, The Staff of Levy, and was dedicated in 1896.

Q: What is the Matte Levy society?

A: They were a group of Jews, *landsmen*, who purchased this section in the cemetery. But it was the date that interested me more than the name. This section was dedicated in 1896. My great-great-grandfather died before anyone was buried here.

Q: So, the search goes on!

A: Yes, and the name of the society also spurred me on. It just so happened that the words *Matte Levi* appeared in that week's Torah portion! "Surely," I said to myself, "this is no coincidence. It is a sign from heaven!"

Somehow, I just had to find the right section. I was on an emotional roller coaster and would not have been surprised if Eliyahu Hanavi had tapped me on the shoulder and directed me to Harav Yaakov Moshe's grave. Since that did not happen, I made my way to the cemetery office.

The woman behind the desk handed me a pile of thick, dusty ledgers. They were handwritten records, each line written in a very difficult-to-read old-fashioned cursive script. How in the world, I wondered, was I going to find his name in all this. I thought it might have been easier to go back into the hot sun and just examine each one of the thousands of graves one at a time! But the office was air-conditioned, and I decided to stay put. I started with the ledger from 1881, knowing that my great-great-grandfather would not have been in America before the murder of Czar

Alexander II in that year. I quickly discovered that I did not have to decipher each name. I knew that my great-great-grandfather must have been at least sixty when he died, so I just skimmed down the age column, which was very easy to read. Very few people made it to their sixties. Most adults only lived into their forties or fifties. My grandfather's case was typical. His father died when he was still a young man, and before he was married. There must have been thousands like him. How many children never knew grandparents! No wonder Judaism fared so badly in America; there was no continuity!

I discovered another sad fact; there were years when it seemed that 95 percent of the entries were children under the age of two. How many families were broken apart by the disease rampant on the Lower East Side? I wondered what role this had played in the breakdown of tradition and the tragedy of American Jewish life. It was getting late; my search through the ledgers was drawing a blank. Reluctantly, I returned them to the clerk, thanking her for her assistance.

I returned to my great-grandparents' graves. I photographed the monuments, and recited a few chapters of *Tehillim*, including Chapter 147, which we say each day. One of the verses in this chapter seemed particularly relevant at this moment: "He Who gives snow like fleece; He scatters frost like ashes. He hurls His ice like crumbs — before His cold, who can stand? He issues His command, and it melts them. He blows His wind, the waters flow."

The next morning, as I recited these words in shul, I knew that I hadn't gotten to where I was from nowhere. "These words," I reminded myself, "were also recited daily by my great-grandparents, my great-great-grandparents, my great-great-great-grandparents and all the generations that came before."

I was no longer a Jew without a past. These words bonded me to them. For forty years, since my great-grandmother's death, the waters of Torah were completely frozen over for the entire family. How did I find the wherewithal to find my way back home? The traditions were not dead; they were like the snow, the frost and the ice. Although for a time frozen, the faith of our fathers was always there, waiting for the first signs of spring. What does the future hold?

"He issues His command, and it melts them.

"He blows His wind, the waters flow."

16

"My Long-Lost Cousin"

Q: You said you were the only observant Jew in your extended family, but I have met your Cousin Bernie, and he is a delightful *kippa*-wearing Jew.

A: Bernie is actually my mother's cousin. His aunt is my grandmother. He has no connection to my grandfather's side. Actually, I didn't know him until quite a few years after I became *frum*, and it was great fun getting to know him. Everyone should have a long-lost cousin.

In late 1991, my mother was in the hospital when

her Aunt Bella died. Aunt Bella was my grandmother's sister. My grandmother also had a brother, George. Because my grandmother did not have a close relationship with them, we knew virtually nothing about them or their children. My mother felt very badly about not being able to go to her funeral, so I offered to go to represent the family.

I arrived at the funeral parlor. I looked around, trying to find a familiar face. There were not too many people I recognized. Finally, I saw my Aunt Wilma and walked over to where she was standing. Most of the men were wearing those horrible pointy shiny silk yarmulkes that they hand out at non-religious Jewish *simchas* or funerals. I noticed one fellow wearing a *kippa* that actually seemed to belong on his head.

Motioning to indicate the fellow in question, I asked my Aunt Wilma, "Who's that?"

"That's my Uncle George's son, Cousin Bernie," she replied.

I wanted to go over to introduce myself, but it wasn't befitting to do so during the ceremony. I looked for him after the service had ended, but he had already left. I accompanied the family to the cemetery.

After the burial, Aunt Bella's son offered to take Bernie's father home.

That's not appropriate, I thought. *He just lost his mother! He shouldn't be running a taxi service.*

And so, I offered to give him a ride.

Once we were on our way, I started my interrogation.

"Uncle George," I asked, "did anyone on your side of the family become religious?"

"Yeah," he said with a sigh, "my son. He prays three times a day. He only eats kosher food, and if his own mother or father would call him on a Saturday, it would be too much for him to pick up the phone. You might call him a real fanatic! What about your side of the family?"

My great-uncle George knew nothing about my family. He probably thought that I was wearing a *kippa* just because of the funeral.

"I have to tell you, Uncle George," I ventured, "that I pray three times a day. I only eat kosher food, and if my own mother or father would call me on a Saturday, it would be too much for me to pick up the phone. You might call me a real fanatic!"

"I would! I would!" he exclaimed almost shouting. "You're both fanatics! You should meet each other."

"Uncle George," I said, "I can't wait to meet your son!"

We arrived at my great-uncle's building, and I wrote my telephone number on a slip of paper for him to give to Bernie.

One evening, a few weeks later, the phone rang. It was Bernie. We talked for hours on end comparing notes and life experiences. We were especially interested in how the other became *frum*. It turned out that we both started keeping Shabbos at about the same time, and we had both attended courses at Lincoln Square Synagogue. Our stories were not identical, but there were an uncanny number of similarities.

Before Bernie and I finally ended our long getting-to-know-you conversation, he said, "Talking to you has been a little like looking in the mirror."

Upon reflection, I replied, "I know exactly what you mean."

When I told the Zs about my new-found cousin, they said without hesitation, "Invite him over for Shabbos. We've got to meet him."

I called him, and he agreed. We set the date for a few weeks later.

However, my grandfather died the Shabbos before we were set to meet, and so we met for the second time, not around the Shabbos table, but at another funeral.

The following week, he came to the Zs. It was a bittersweet Shabbos — my first without my grandfather. However, it was a great comfort to have found a family member with whom I had something in common, someone with whom I could share being Jewish. Over the next few months, Bernie and I became the best of friends.

About a year later, I moved to Eretz Yisrael. Bernie was very upset. He told me, "It isn't fair. I just got to know you, and now you are moving half way across the world." However, our friendship has withstood the test of distance. Since my aliya, Bernie has made quite a few trips here. He spends his vacation time in Israel doing volunteer work. He takes a break from his arduous work to come to us for Shabbos, relaxing (if it can be called that) with our small children who adore their Cousin Bernie.

17

"My Heart Is in the East"

Q: It's a long way from Flushing to Eretz Yisrael where you, your wife, and your adorable children are living. How long after you became *frum* did you start contemplating a move to Eretz Yisrael, and what caused you to make your final decision?

A: I started thinking about Eretz Yisrael not only before I was *frum*, but even while I yet identified as a Christian. Once I saw that Holocaust documentary in ninth grade, I became fascinated with the Jewish people. The idea of their return to Eretz Yisrael captivated me. The building up of

Israel, the ingathering of her people, her tenacity, and her courage filled me with awe. Although I still considered myself a Christian, I somehow wished that I could be a part of it.

I remember when I was in my last year at the Polytechnic Institute of New York. The President of Israel, Ephraim Katzir, came to speak to the Jewish students. Though I was already rarely going to church, I was not a member of any Jewish student organization, either, so I don't know why I was invited. However, I was intrigued, and so I went.

President Katzir told us that we were soon to become engineers, and he was sure that we would all contribute to society. "In America," he said, "you will be cogs in the wheel. America will manage nicely without your contributions. In Israel, however, we need you. You can make a difference." His words made a great impression on me.

Israel always had magic for me, and, as I became more connected to the Jewish people, it was always at the back of my mind as a place to live. Once I started on my journey home, there was no question in my mind; it was the next logical step for me.

To be a better Jew, I had to start keeping kashrut, and then...

To be a better Jew, I had to keep Shabbos, and then...

To be a better Jew, I had to live in a Jewish community, and then…

To be a better Jew, I had to go to yeshiva, I had to learn, and then…

To be a better Jew, I had to live in Eretz Yisrael.

Q: Yet today, most Jews in the diaspora don't even consider living in Eretz Yisrael high on their list of priorities.

A: Let me tell you a story. When I was working at Sperry, there was a very clever young man in our department. One day, around Pesach time, John, a non-Jew, came over to me, newspaper in hand. He said, "I was just reading an article here about Passover. It says that at the end of your seder, you guys say, 'Next year in Jerusalem!' Well, what about it? Are you guys serious or what?"

It took me a moment or two to decide how I should answer. "You have to understand," I ventured, "that it means something more than the simple words convey. It expresses our hope that next year the world will be the way it was supposed to be — with no wars and no strife."

John wasn't going to let me off the hook so easily.

With a sly smile, he asked, "But it also means what it says, doesn't it?"

And of course, there he had me. And he knew it.

"It does mean what it says, but you have to understand," I answered defensively, "life is not always so simple. To move to Israel means coping with a different language and a different culture, leaving family and friends, and finding a job. It's not something you can just pick up and do in a moment."

"I don't understand you guys," he said. "I see that when we go on business trips, you have to arrange to find someone to host you for Shabbos. You lug along your cans of tuna fish to make sure you have kosher food. You ask for problems at work by taking off early on Fridays. I know that instead of relaxing in front of the television set in the evenings, you're sitting and breaking your heads over some obscure passage that some rabbis wrote thousands of years ago. Nothing is too hard for you Jews! So tell me, why is this so hard?"

There was nothing to say. I knew he was right — and that's why I eventually found my way here to Eretz Yisrael.

Q: And so here you are. How did you get here?

A: My first attempt was in 1989. I came to Israel armed with names of yeshivot that I was told might be suitable. My plan was to leave my job and to come and learn full-time. My dear friend Yoni, who was married and living in Jerusalem, made arrangements for me to spend Shabbos in Rabbi Bulman's community, Kiryat Nachliel, in Migdal HaEmek. That Shabbos happened to be the tenth anniversary of the community, and Rabbi Zev Leff had been invited as the scholar-in-residence.

It was the first time I heard Rav Leff speak. He gave a dynamic *derasha* on the weekly parasha. The parasha for that week was *Lech Lecha*! Can you imagine?

"*Hashem* told Avram," Rav Leff explained, "leave your country. There, you will always remain an Avram. There, you will never reach your potential. For you to be an Avraham, you need to be in Eretz Yisrael."

I felt he was speaking directly to me. I knew that to reach my potential as a Jew, I had to be in Eretz Yisrael. If it hadn't been Shabbos, I might have called Lou and quit my job on the spot.

After the Shabbos meal, I sat with Rabbi Bulman and told him of my plans to leave work and enroll in a yeshiva in Israel.

"Can you recommend a place that would be right for me? Where do you think I should go?" I asked him intently.

"Where should you go?" he repeated. "I think you should stay put!"

"What? Stay put?" I asked in amazement. "Why should I stay put? You're a rabbi, and you are actually telling me not to take time out to learn in a yeshiva? I don't understand."

"You should stay put!" he said emphatically, almost shouting.

I was hurt. I was disappointed. I was even, to put it mildly, angry. I had expected a little more encouragement.

"But Rabbi Bulman, there are so many things I need to know. Yoni told you about my background. I am starting from zero. I have come a long way, but I will never learn what I need to know so long as I have only the evening hours to study. In other words, you are telling me: You can go this far, and no further!"

"Listen," he said to me gently, "you are not a college kid. You are already in your thirties. Your first priority now has to be to find a *shidduch*. You must devote your efforts to building a family. Before you make any move, you have to ask yourself how it will affect your chances of finding a wife."

"In the States," he went on, "you have good connections. I know the Zs from when I was a rabbi there. They are wonderful people, and I know they'll help you. If you come here, few people will know you. You will have to establish yourself all over again. Your job now is to find a wife, and not to come here."

"But what about learning in a yeshiva? I really feel that I must learn full time," I told him.

He said with a sigh, "I understand, but your profession is in hi-tech. You need to retain your profession so that you can support a family. I am sure that your family would not support you in order for you to learn full time. Once you leave your profession, who knows if you will be able to return to it? How will you manage?"

"I just want to do it for a year," I persisted. "After a year, I will find an engineering job here."

"You say now that it will be for a year," he answered patiently, "but I have no doubt that at the end of the year, you will want to stay. That year will turn into two years, and then three and then four. You won't be able to go back to your profession."

He must have noticed my downcast face.

"Don't be so upset," he comforted me. "You are doing very well learning at night in the yeshiva in Queens. I can tell you that you are doing much better than many boys who are learning full time here in Eretz Yisrael. You are progressing nicely, and that is why I advising you to stay put."

Q: This must have been a crushing disappointment.

A: It certainly wasn't the answer I expected. When I told other people what Rabbi Bulman had said, the reaction was, "Rabbi Bulman said that? Maybe you misunderstood him." They assured me, "Just trust in Hashem, take the jump and things will work out!"

Q: Did you, and did it?

A: No, I listened to Rabbi Bulman and stayed at my job. I decided that, at least for the next few years, I would remain in America and make building a family my top priority. Although I was disappointed, I knew in my heart that Rabbi Bulman was right.

When I eventually did come, he and his rebbetzin helped me tremendously. For two years, I lived not far from them in Jerusalem and became a *ben bayis* by them. In my early years in Israel, whenever I had a problem, whenever I needed advice, he was the first person I turned to.

Rabbi Bulman's greatness was that he never gave one-size-fits-all answers. He had a keen eye for analyzing a situation and getting to the core of the matter, and he always spoke the truth.

Anyway, I returned to America. I made tremendous efforts to find my *shidduch*, but to no avail. One day, while walking down Queens Boulevard in Flushing, I was stopped by a man who handed me a pamphlet entitled, "*Metziat Zivug*, Finding Your Mate."

"Do you have this one?" he asked.

"The pamphlet, I have," I answered. "It's the *zivug* I'm missing!"

In 1991, my grandfather's health was deteriorating. I was glad I had remained in America. He needed me, and I also needed him. But, by January 1992, he was gone.

With my grandfather's passing and no *shidduch* in sight, my thoughts again turned to moving to Eretz Yisrael.

I put my apartment up for sale, but the New York

real estate market had collapsed. The price I could get exceeded the money I owed the bank. My friend, Mark, suggested that I rent it out.

"How am I going to rent out an apartment from Israel?" I asked.

"If that is what is preventing you from moving, don't worry. I'll take care of it for you until you can sell it."

Q: How were you going to support yourself? It costs a lot of money to make aliya. There are shipping costs, the cost of setting up a new home, oh a million and one things! Weren't you worried about the finances?

A: I was, but once again *hashgacha* stepped in. They had a big layoff at work. I wasn't laid off, but the union rules allowed for people to volunteer for the layoff and thus be eligible for a generous severance package. If I were to volunteer, I would easily be able to manage for at least a few months.

Those who were laid off were given two weeks notice. Anyone who wanted to volunteer had one week to decide. Despite all my plans and dreams, it was not an easy decision; but, I knew that it was now or never.

Q: That was brave. How old were you then?

A: It was in 1993, so I was thirty-four years old. During the week that I had to decide, I must have changed my mind several times each day.

Q: You suggested at one point in our discussion that your whole life as a *baal teshuva* was full of *hashgacha*. Where was the *hashgacha* at this time?

A: Well, obviously, the *hashgacha* was that I was given this opportunity to come to Israel.

Q: And nothing else? There were no other signs?

A: Well, a voice did not come from the heavens, saying, "*Lech Lecha!*" But I knew that a decision not to come would, in a sense, be a betrayal of all the struggles that had gone before. I was at a turning point, and I was very nervous. Decision Monday was just a few days away, and I couldn't make up my mind. Sunday morning, I woke up and said to myself, "This is it! Tomorrow I will sign the forms and volunteer for the layoff."

As the day progressed, to my surprise, I remained firm and comfortable with my decision. That evening, I went to a fund-raising dinner for the yeshiva. In his speech, the rosh yeshiva addressed his *talmidim*, saying, "You have to strive to be a better Jew. Tomorrow needs to be different. You have to get out of your rut! You have to move forward."

After his speech, the *rosh yeshiva* approached me. "Well," he said, "tomorrow is the big day. What will you do?"

"I'm going to sign the papers. I'm going to go to Eretz Yisrael!" I replied.

"What finally made you decide?" he asked.

I looked him straight in the eye and said without missing a beat, "Your speech!"

He turned as white as a sheet.

"My speech? You don't have to listen to me. The boys in the yeshiva often don't listen to me! Are you sure? You need to weigh all the issues very carefully. Don't decide on the basis of my speech!" he said with panic in his voice.

"Sorry," I said. "I was only kidding. I decided this morning. Your speech was very good, but it had nothing to do with it."

Monday morning, I arrived at work. Lou was on vacation, so I walked over to my immediate supervisor's desk.

"Mike," I said, "I would like a copy of the forms to volunteer for the layoff."

"You're joking," he said. "In this tight job market, who would volunteer for a layoff?"

"I'm not joking," I said, "so please give me the forms."

"What?" he asked, "Do you have a job offer from somewhere else?"

"No," I replied, "I'm moving to Israel."

"You are joking!" he said, "Come on, let's get back

to work. I had an interesting idea for the fingerprinting algorithm…"

"I'm not joking, Mike. Please give me the forms."

He looked up at me. His expression turned serious.

"You're not joking," he said. "I don't understand you. I don't understand how anyone could leave his country, especially an American. People are lining up to get here, and you want to leave? You really would do that?"

I decided not to answer him. How could I explain to a non-Jew the power and relevance of Hashem's command to Avraham, "*Lech Lecha* — leave your homeland and travel to the land I will show you"?

He gave me the forms, and I signed them, and handed them in at the end of the day. I drove home, parked the car, and walked through the courtyard to enter the building. I went up the one flight of stairs, unlocked both locks on the door, opened it, and entered my home of the last six years. I closed the door behind me, leaned against it, took a deep breath and said, "What have I done?"

18

"On My Way"

Q: What do you mean, "What have I done?" You had burned all your bridges behind you, that's what you had done. But why were you so upset? Wasn't this what you had dreamed of for years?

A: Yes, but now it wasn't a dream. I had to face the reality that I was really going. I wouldn't say that I was upset, but I *was* nervous. I wasn't sure I would succeed, but I was determined to give it my best try.

Q: What about your family? How did they take this decision?

A: I called home and spoke with my mother. I said hesitantly, "I-I've made a decision."

"What now?" my mother asked.

"I've quit my job."

"You did what?"

"I've quit my job," I repeated.

"You quit your job?" my mother echoed in disbelief. "Why would you do that? I thought you loved your job. You told me that the work is interesting, that you enjoy being with the people you work with, and that you get along well with your boss. Did something happen?"

"Umm...not exactly. I wasn't fired or anything, but I think it's time, how shall we say, to look for new opportunities."

"Well, I certainly hope you didn't quit your job without having a new one in hand."

"Actually, I don't have anything in hand at the moment," I said.

"So why on earth did you quit your job?" she asked.

"For the standard reasons. I'm moving to Israel!"

"You're moving to where?"

"To Israel!"

"You're moving to Israel? Do you want to kill me?"

"No, of course I don't want to kill you, but this is something I have been thinking about for years."

"So why not think about it for a few more years?" she asked with a sigh.

"It's now or never. I'm sure this is not a complete surprise to you."

"You are moving so far away. We'll never see our grandchildren!"

"But Mom," I said, "I'm not even married. You don't even have any grandchildren from me to worry about."

"But you will get married, and you will have children, and we will never know them."

"Why don't we cross that bridge when and if we come to it," I said, trying to console her. "I'm sure that if I do get married and have children, you will be very happy, even if you don't get to see them very often."

"Listen," my mother said with another sigh, "we raised all of you children to do what you think is right. If you think this is right, how can we stand in your way?"

My parents were not thrilled with my decision, but, as always, they were supportive. I am sure that they were proud that I was acting on my convictions.

A day or two after my decision, during my last week at work, Lou returned from his vacation. I went into his office to break the news. He said, "Good for you! Israel is one heck of a country. They have a lot of guts. I just can't help wondering, though, if it'll be here in fifty years. They have so many enemies!"

"Listen, Lou," I said, "the odds for our survival haven't been very good for over two thousand years. But with G-d's help, we're still here."

"Well," he said, "I really wish you a lot of luck. I've enjoyed working with you for the past nine years. Drop us a line from time to time to let us know how you're doing."

My colleagues made a little party for me at the end of the week, I packed up my things, and that was that.

The following Monday was Pesach. As usual, I was at the Zs. We had a lovely seder, and everyone was talking, saying, "Just like the Jewish people left Egypt, now you are leaving your Egypt. Hopefully, we won't be far behind."

We finished very late, and after I finally fell asleep, I dreamed that I had decided not to take the layoff. In my dream, I felt very angry and disappointed with myself. I woke up in a cold sweat. The dream was so vivid that for a few moments, I wasn't even sure if I had quit or not. I had to think, *Yes, I remember handing in the forms. Yes, I remember the farewell party. I remember getting my last paycheck, and I certainly remember my mother's reaction. Yes, phew, I did quit.*

A few days after Pesach, I found out about a pilot trip that was being offered by the Tehilla organization. I missed the registration deadline, but they agreed to let me join the trip anyway.

Q: What is Tehilla?

A: Tehilla is a religious organization, staffed by wonderful people, that helps potential immigrants. Not only do they help people find employment, they also help the new immigrant integrate into Israeli society.

Q: Where are they? In America or Israel?

A: The main office is in Israel, but they have branches not only in America but also in many western countries.

Q: How I wish there had been a Tehilla when I made my first aliya from London in 1974. Perhaps if they had been around, I would not have had to endure my second aliya and then my third! But, *baruch Hashem*, finally I made it my way.

A: When I joined the pilot trip, they set up dozens of interviews for me. Sometimes I had three interviews in a single day. It was exhausting.

Nevertheless, no one offered me a job. The most

positive response I received was, "Call us after you have made aliya."

I was very discouraged.

The pilot trip came to an end. I delayed my return to America to continue my job search. During that time, I stayed with Yoni in Jerusalem. He not only offered me a place to sleep, but also offered me constant encouragement and practical advice.

Although the pilot trip was officially over, the staff of Tehilla continued to arrange interviews for me. One was at Motorola in Tel Aviv. Everyone told me it was a great company to work for, and I was very excited. My interview with Gadi went very well, and I even held my own in Hebrew. I returned to Jerusalem feeling very optimistic, and I was delighted when, a day or two later, I was invited back.

I would have preferred that this interview be conducted in English, but I didn't make a fuss when they began to speak in Hebrew.

They asked me how I would go about solving a particular problem. I told them, but from the look on their faces, I realized that I had misunderstood their question and had thought they had posed a far more complicated problem. When I realized my mistake, I lost all self-confidence and completely flubbed the next two questions. They didn't bother to ask me any more questions. The interview came to an abrupt end.

An embarrassed Gadi escorted a humiliated me to the lobby. "We'll be in touch," he mumbled.

Sure, I thought as I walked smack into the glass door. I rubbed my nose, adjusted my eyeglasses, and, with as much composure as I could muster, I fled from the scene.

Q: What a terrible beginning!

A: I returned to Jerusalem in very low spirits. I decided to stop off and walk around Geula and Meah Shearim. Strolling around these neighborhoods, among religious Jews, always had an attraction for me, and I thought it might cheer me up

Q: I know what the attraction is for me, but what is the attraction for you?

A: I don't know. The neighborhood has a very unique atmosphere. It is both a commercial center and spiritual center. On the one hand, there is the hustle and bustle of the shops. At the same time, you can feel the *kedusha* there as well. On each narrow side street or alleyway are dozens of little yeshivot, *shtieblech* and *sefarim* stores. I love standing underneath the windows of the *chedarim* to hear the little boys learning in their sweet sing-song voices.

I entered a pizza shop, and, like a good American, waited my turn to be served. Everyone pushed ahead of me. I thought I wasn't being served because I wasn't one of them. and, in disgust, I turned around and left.

By the time I returned to Yoni's apartment, I was angry at the world.

"How was your day?" Yoni innocently inquired.

I scowled and said, "Awful. I stopped off in Geula on my way back. No one there would give me the time of day, much less a slice of pizza.

"I guess the interview didn't go too well, did it?" he asked.

"No, it didn't. I almost broke my nose and my glasses."

I told him what had happened.

"You'll find a job. Don't worry."

"I don't know, Yoni. I quit my job, there's nothing to go back to in America, and who knows if I'll ever find a job here."

"Look," he told me, "living here is not like living in America. The Torah says of Eretz Yisrael, 'The eyes of Hashem are on it from the beginning of the year till the end of the year.' Now, of course Hashem sees everything in all places. The *pasuk* is telling us that there is a special *hashgacha* in Eretz Yisrael. You can't plan too far ahead here, and you shouldn't even try. The way it works is that you get what you need, but only when you need it. If you don't get it, then you don't need it."

Yoni's advice and encouragement has remained

Q: with me ever since, and I repeat his words to other people who are contemplating aliya.

Q: I, too, discovered the uniqueness of Eretz Yisrael. The kindness found here cannot be duplicated anywhere else. People are genuinely concerned about your well-being.

A: Yes, there is a feeling that we are all family here. Let me tell you a rather funny story that illustrates this.

The experts at Tehilla suggested that I open a bank account during the pilot trip to make things easier later on.

I went to the main branch of one of the banks in Jerusalem. The woman on the other side of the desk looked like a typical Jewish grandmother. She started to write down my details.

"Name?"

I gave her my name.

"Address?"

I gave her my address.

"Date of birth?"

I told her.

"Marital Status?"

"Single."

"Single?" she said, looking up at me over her eyeglasses. "We'll have to fix that. We're a full-service bank."

Q: You just made that up, didn't you?

A: No, it really did happen. It would be unbelievable anywhere else, but here, I don't think it's all that surprising. I told the folks at Tehilla what she said, and they told me, "Don't worry. We're trying to fix you up too!"

Tehilla also organized visits to different communities for the pilot trip participants. This was more relevant to families who were trying to decide where to live, but I enjoyed these trips as well. We went to quite a few communities in Yehuda and the Shomron, beyond the green line.

On one of these trips, I was looking out the window of our bus, daydreaming, when Chaim, one of the organizers, sat down in the empty seat next to me. Chaim was very active in the settlement movement.

"What do you think?" he said. "It's impressive what we've built here, isn't it?"

"Yes," I said, "I'm impressed. Such beautiful communities have been built from nothing. However, I'm also worried. I see these little settlements, some with only a few dozen houses, hanging on to the side of a hill, and I see how vulnerable they are. They could be wiped off the map, *chas veshalom*, in a moment."

"What?" he said in agitation. "Are you some kind of a heretic? Don't you believe that Hashem brought us back here and that He will protect us? This is the beginning of the redemption!"

"Listen, Chaim," I said, "I'm not a heretic, and I also believe that the *geula* will come, but I don't presume to know what will happen as we go from Point A to Point B. So when I see how vulnerable these places are, it worries me."

"You have to have faith," he told me. "There may be bumps in the road, but these are just minor distractions. The Arabs tried to defeat us with their *intifada*, but they soon saw that their sticks and stones were no match for us, and they gave up. The Left thought we were beaten, but Hashem had other plans."

I saw that Chaim was a true believer, hoped he was right, and we didn't discuss it any further.

Little did either of us know that the Oslo Accords were in the making, and a new more vicious *intifada*, with rifles and suicide bombers, would come in their wake.

Q: This brings me to a topic that greatly worries me — the dangerous influences of Christian evangelicals on Israel in general and on the settler movement in particular. A lot of people tell me that I am paranoid and don't know what I am talking about. You grew up among these Christians, so tell me, am I paranoid or not?

A: Just because you are paranoid doesn't mean that someone out there isn't trying to get you. But seriously, I agree with you that there is a real danger.

Let me tell you how Christians go about getting a Jew to convert. They set their sights on lonely people, people going through a crisis. They try to become their friend. They lend a listening ear. They don't start talking about their beliefs right away — first comes the softening up process. After they gain the person's confidence, they start to tell them about how they also once had troubles, and how letting their so-called savior into their lives helped them. The Jew is more receptive now. After all, in his eyes, this is not a missionary talking; it is his friend, with his best interests at heart.

I am convinced that a similar process is underway here in Israel.

Our brothers in the territories are under siege. About half the country views them as an obstacle to peace. Most of the world despises them. The settlers are convinced that the whole Oslo process was a ruse, a Trojan horse. People wanted so badly to believe that peace with the Arabs was possible, that they let the enemy into the gates. What many of the settlers don't realize is that they themselves have let another Trojan horse into the city, and this horse contains a far more sophisticated and dangerous enemy. The terrorists endanger our lives; these Christians endanger our souls.

The Christians come along offering to help, not with missionary intentions — oh no, not them. They find Jews, isolated, in crisis, in need of financial, emotional and political support and offer to help, no strings attached. This is the softening up process. One of the largest cities in the Shomron has gotten a huge sum of money from the Christians. Is it any surprise that a messianic Jewish congregation is now active there?

Not long ago, I discovered that a Christian group had instructed its readers to write letters that would be forwarded by the group to Jews in Israel. "Don't mention J.," the instructions warned. "Save that for subsequent letters should you succeed in maintaining a correspondence with someone."

I know them from the inside, and I know what they are up to.

Q: But you told me that they are not monsters, that they are not all evil.

A: They have their agenda. Perhaps their intentions are up for debate, but for us it really doesn't matter. They are out to rip us away from our traditions. And we need to protect ourselves and have nothing to do with them.

Q: They speak of reconciliation, building bridges.

A: Reconciliation to what? They use this as a code

word. They want us to be reconciled to their beliefs. Building bridges? They want a one-way bridge. They want us to come to them.

Q: I once interviewed the leader of a Pentecostal church operating in Israel. He thought I was a Christian journalist writing for a Christian newspaper. He also explained to me that his job was to help Jews cross the bridge.

A: They want to break down our resistance to them. In the old days, a Jew wouldn't go near one of their bridges! And I can tell you that it is not only the settlers. Everyone is falling for the temptation of their money. The government chastises American Jewish fund-raising efforts for highlighting the poverty here, but at the same time, they are gratefully accepting money from the Christians to supplement dwindling social budgets. And it doesn't stop there. They are even financing the aliya of *olim* from Russia.

And they are succeeding in "building bridges."

Recently, we had a couple visiting us for Shabbos whose aliya was partially funded by Christians. They told us, "The Christians are not all that bad. If they are willing to give us money, why shouldn't we take it?" Now, I don't think that this young *chareidi* couple is about to become Christian, but the barrier has been lowered, and the constant favorable press highlighting Christian aid and generosity does affect how Israeli society views Christianity. The taboo has been broken.

There is another danger. Eventually their hidden agenda will become less and less hidden. Sooner or later, they will make demands on us that we won't be able to meet — just as with the Palestinians when it became clear to most people that we had been hoodwinked. After having received so much money and so much political support from the Christians, telling them "this far and no further," would be tantamount to spurning their "love." Then the face full of hatred, so familiar to us throughout the centuries, will replace the smiling face we see now.

Neither your honey nor your sting! But it's hard to reject the people who seem to be our only friends in the world.

Q: You sound deeply concerned about the situation.

A: I certainly am. One of the reasons I wanted to move to Israel is because I wanted to live in a place free of Christian influences. I am very uneasy about all these well-meaning Jews who are foolishly relying on Christian support for short-term gain.

Anyway, my pilot trip was drawing to a close. I had no job in America, and no job offers in Israel, but there was turning back on my decision. I was determined to make a go of it.

Q: I read that Rabbi Dessler felt that by visiting the holy land, every Jew would then be able to appreciate this wonderful land and understand why

Hashem chose it for us. But he warned that a Jew should not come first for a trial period. He said, "Only those who come determined to stay, without any calculations and questions, with *mesiras nefesh*, and ready to suffer, remain."*

A: I often think that if I had fully thought out the difficulties of my aliya before I came, I never would have come.

I tried to internalize Yoni's advice to me: "You'll get what you need when you need it, and if you don't get it, you don't need it."

The day before I was scheduled to leave, I got a call from Tehilla. There was a small company in Jerusalem that wanted to interview me the next day. I thought it was a little silly to go to yet another interview hours before my flight, but I decided to go anyway.

Q: And they offered you a job on the spot!

A: No. The interview went well, but they made no promises. I returned to America, packed up my things, bought my appliances, and found a tenant for my apartment. I submitted my application to the aliya center in New York, and got my immigrant visa. I was very nervous, but determined to give it my best shot.

---

* Rav Dessler. *The Life and Impact of Rabbi Eliahu Eliezer Dessler, the Mictav Me'Eliyahu*, Yonoson Rosenblum, Mesorah Publications Ltd., May 2000, page 261.

A few weeks before I was about to leave, I received a phone call from the company where I interviewed during the last few hours of my pilot trip, saying, "We'd like you to come to work for us."

They made a salary offer, and I calmly told them I would think it over and get back to them.

I hung up the phone, jumped a few feet in the air, and yelped, "I have a job offer in Jerusalem!"

My parents came to visit me in Flushing the day before I was scheduled to leave. We decided that an airport parting would be too hard for everyone concerned. We stood in my now almost empty apartment as we said our good-byes.

"Your father and I," my mother said, "want you to be happy. We wish that something else would make you happy. But if this is what you believe you must do, then do it."

Our parting was difficult. I love my parents very much. They do not understand why I need to be here, but I think I have the most understanding parents in the world.

The next day the Zs took me to the airport. I thanked them for all their help over the years.

"We'll see you soon," they said. "We're right behind you!" And sure enough, nine years later they also came on aliya.

The plane took off. I was leaving my family and

friends far behind. I sat there in my seat, looking out the window, with tears in my eyes. But as the flight progressed, my spirits picked up. I was on my way home.

19

"Coming Home"

Q: I'm sure you probably have dozens and dozens of stories of your experiences from your first years of aliya. Perhaps you can tell us one or two that are most meaningful to you.

A: The events surrounding the kidnapping of Nachshon Wachsman, *hy"d*, by Arab terrorists made an enormous impression on me. His kidnapping generated an unprecedented feeling of unity that gripped the entire nation, and together we held our breath, hoping and praying for his release. Through the media exposure, we learned more about Nachshon, and soon everyone either became his mother, father, brother or friend. With their unshakable faith and quiet dignity, his parents became pillars of strength for the nation. I heard on the radio about a school in Rechovot where, when it came time for recess, the children refused to go out and play. "We want to stay inside and pray for Nachshon," they told their teacher.

After the terrorists released the video of him in captivity, feelings of rage, hopelessness and powerlessness seized us all. His parents told us that we were not powerless, that there was something we could do to help their son. They requested that all of us, religious, non-religious, men, women and children go to the Western Wall to recite *Tehillim* and prayers on his behalf.

On Thursday night, fifty thousand of us gathered at the Western Wall. Every group was represented. Nachshon's high school principal led the service. Tears were streaming down our faces as we recited *Tehillim*, which seemed to be written just for this occasion. There was a tremendous unity of purpose. I had arrived at the *Kotel* depressed over the situation, but I left strengthened by being among so many of our people. I was sure that Hashem would see our unity, and answer our prayers.

Early on Friday, the announcement came that Rabin, Peres and Arafat had won the Nobel Peace Prize. It seemed like a cruel joke. Friday afternoon, I went to a kibbutz between Jerusalem and Tel

Aviv. Nathan and Dina's daughter, Batsheva, had come on aliya about a year after my arrival, and Batsheva's husband Aaron was in the *kollel* there. As Shabbos arrived, we went to daven knowing that the deadline that Nachson's captors had set was near. The next morning, a small group gathered in front of the *beis medrash*, speaking in hushed tones. A non-Jewish worker had passed on the information that he had heard on the radio, that Nachshon, along with one of his would-be rescuers, had been killed in the attempt to free him.

I went outside and just stood for a while. I felt as if something inside of me had broken.

Nachson's mother was from Queens, where I had lived before coming to Israel. The family had lived in my neighborhood in Jerusalem before moving to Ramot. So many of my neighbors knew the family. A friend of mine had rented an apartment from them. Although I did not know Nachshon or his family, I felt that I had lost someone close to me. Aaron and I waited till after Shabbos to tell the others the sad news.

After Shabbos, I returned to Jerusalem. The funeral was set for midnight. Eli, a friend of mine from work, called me up and asked me if I needed a ride. People were coming to the cemetery, by foot and by cars, from all over the city. Eli saw that we would never make it in time, but he had lived nearby and was familiar with the area. We drove through the back streets of Bayit VeGan, and from there we walked to the cemetery. The streams of people coming from all directions soon became rivers of Jews, expressionless, numb, all making their way to Mount Herzl determined to demonstrate their feelings and respect for Nachshon and his family.

A few days before, we had gathered at the *Kotel* full of hope, and now, again, tens of thousands of us were gathered to accompany Nachshon to his final resting place. Nachson's principal again spoke, but this time it was to eulogize Nachshon. As he spoke and described Nachshon, one could hear the sobbing of those who had come to know him in the last few days. He described how this young man had brought together the entire nation. Over the loudspeakers, one could hear the sounds of the shovels and the thump of the earth as Nachshon was buried. The crowds dispersed, and we went home. I finally went to bed at about three in the morning, but I couldn't sleep.

During the week of shiva, Nachshon's mother issued a statement. She wanted the world to know that the family's faith was not diminished by the events of the previous Shabbos. We don't understand why things turned out the way they did, she said, but we know that G-d is a G-d of mercy and love. He is our Father, and sometimes a father says no.

The experience of those few weeks made me feel connected to the Jewish people in a way that would not have been possible had I remained in America.

Another story that I must tell you is about a trip I made with Eli to Hebron. Eli was not only my colleague at work; he quickly became one of my closest friends. Especially in my first years here, whenever I was a little down, he cheered me up. He introduced me to his friends, and to this day, we meet whenever we can.

Eli suggested that we go one Friday morning to daven in Hebron. I agreed, and was looking forward to seeing Hebron for the first time.

We boarded the bus in Jerusalem a few hours before dawn, and traveled to Hebron while it was still dark. As the bus turned from the main road into the narrow streets of the city, the eastern sky began to lighten. When we arrived, the large structure of the Cave of the Patriarchs was silhouetted against the softly glowing sky. I was overcome with emotion. I felt as if I were visiting the graves, not of historical figures, but the graves of my grandparents. I was stunned, because I had not expect to feel much of anything. We ascended the steps to the entrance and entered one of the halls to daven.

I was trembling as I said the words, *Elokei Avraham, Elokei Yitzchak, Elokei Yaakov*, "the G-d of Avraham, the G-d of Yitzchak, the G-d of Yaakov." I couldn't believe how closely attached I felt to our forefathers.

I thanked Hashem for guiding me throughout the years of my return — for bringing me back to the faith of Avraham, Yitzchak and Yaakov. I thanked

Him for all the *hashgacha pratis* bestowed on me, for sending the right people to me, for bringing me home.

I thanked Hashem for connecting me to my past, and pleaded with Him to give me a future — that He help me find a wife, and enable me to raise a family in Eretz Yisrael.

About a year later, I met Jeannette. Hashem has given us a family, and when I hear my children davening or telling over the parasha, it often brings tears to my eyes. Who could have imagined that I, born a Jew yet raised as a Christian in a small town on Long Island, would make my way back to Eretz Yisrael and raise an observant Jewish family?

Q: So here you are. Surely the hard part is over?

A: Not exactly. It was hard to become a *baal teshuva*, to start following the halacha, to learn what the halacha expects of us. It was also at times difficult to settle here in Israel. Both experiences had a lot in common — the excitement of discovery, the disappointment when reality did not quite meet expectations, and learning to live with the dissonance between the two.

Most of the challenges I faced in becoming a *baal teshuva* were largely technical: learning what was permitted and not permitted on Shabbos, learning about kashrus, learning how to study Gemara. The same was true with the challenges of aliya: learning the language, learning how to cope in a bank, adapting to the Israeli mindset in the workplace.

The challenge I now face in coming home is much more daunting, because it involves changes not so much in what I do, or where I live, but in who I am. How do I become a better husband, a better father, a better son and a better friend — in short a better Jew?

The words of the Torah seem to resonate in my own saga:

> *"There, among the nations where G-d will have banished you, you will reflect on the situation" (Devarim 30:1).*

In my family, we almost lost every vestige of Jewish identity. A school teacher showed an innocent ninth-grader a documentary on the Holocaust, and he reflected on the situation.

> *"You will then return to Hashem, your G-d...." (ibid., 30:2).*

Hashem implanted in my heart a burning desire to learn Hebrew. He sent me Rabbi Goldwasser's *Morning Chizuk* radio program, Rabbi Shimoni, the Bulmans, my *chavrusa* Yoni, and most of all Nathan and Dina Ziv and numerous other emissaries to show me the way.

> *"Even if your diaspora is at the ends of the heavens...G-d...will gather you up from there, and He will take you back" (ibid., 30:4).*

Hashem gathered me from the ends of the heavens — a Baptist church on Long Island. Who could have imagined that a Jew who grew up in that distant place would find his way back? But Hashem gathered me from there, and as if that wasn't enough...

> *"Hashem, your G-d, will then bring you to the land that your ancestors possessed, and you too shall possess it. He will be good to you and make you flourish even more than your ancestors..." (ibid., 30:5).**

Hashem brought me to Israel. He gave me a family. He gave me back my life. My grandmother, although not particularly knowledgeable about our traditions, was right. Her instincts told her that our family's wandering would not last forever, that we would safely make the journey home.